COOK
WRAP
SELL

A GUIDE TO STARTING AND RUNNING A SUCCESSFUL *food business* FROM YOUR KITCHEN

by Bruce McMichael

brightword

A Brightword book | www.brightwordpublishing.com

HARRIMAN HOUSE LTD
3A Penns Road
Petersfield
Hampshire
GU32 2EW
GREAT BRITAIN

Tel: +44 (0)1730 233870 | Fax: +44 (0)1730 233880
Email: enquiries@harriman-house.com | Website: www.harriman-house.com

ISBN: 9781908003270

British Library Cataloguing in Publication Data | A CIP catalogue record for this book can be obtained from the British Library.

Book printed and bound in the UK by CPI Antony Rowe
Set in Caslon and joeHand 2

With many thanks to my children Lucy and Robbie, and my Mother, for their unstinting support and humorous encouragement throughout the writing of this book!

Get the eBook of

COOK WRAP SELL

for free

As a buyer of the printed version of this book you can download the **eBook version** free of charge in formats compatible with Kindle, iPad, Kobo and other eBook readers. Just point your camera or tablet phone at the code above or go to:

ebooks.harriman-house.com/cookwrapsell

Contents

Introduction   xi
    Who this book is for   xi
    What this book does   xii

PART ONE: Starting Your Food Business   1

CHAPTER 1: Cooking up a Great Idea   3
    Starting your home-based food business   5
    Key steps in creating your business   6
    What's your niche?   7
    Research   10

CHAPTER 2: Types of Food Business   21
    Catering   23
    Producer   27

CHAPTER 3: Refining Your Ideas   31
    Focus groups   33
    Cooking schools   40

CHAPTER 4: Planning Your Business   45
    Business plan   47
    Financials   50
    Mentors   57

CHAPTER 5: Costs and Funding 61
Costs 63
Pricing 70
Funding 75

CHAPTER 6: Registering Your Business 83
What's the best form of company for me? 85
Environmental health registration 88
What to call your company and how to protect its name 92

CHAPTER 7: Accountants, Tax and Insurance 99
Accountants and tax 101
Insurance 106
Admin Q&A 109

PART TWO: Running Your Food Business 113

CHAPTER 8: Being a Home-based Business 115
Kitchen layout tips 117
Saving money in the kitchen 122
Health and safety 123
Creating your perfect work environment 128
Getting around 130

CHAPTER 9: Recipes and Ingredients 133
What goes in? 135
Food allergies and intolerances 142

Scaling up production   144
Quality standards and certification   146

CHAPTER 10: Branding and Packaging   149
Design appeal   151
It's a bit like therapy   153
Design brief: a checklist   154
Packaging   155

CHAPTER 11: New Product Development   163
What is new product development (or NPD)?   165
From idea to new product   167
'Tis the season   168
Ethical eating   173

PART THREE: Marketing and Sales   175

CHAPTER 12: Promoting Your Products   177
Impress the press   179
Competitions and promotions   183
Awards   185
Networking   187

CHAPTER 13: Your Business Website   191
Online presence   193
Pages to include   194
Attracting visitors   197
E-commerce tools   199

CHAPTER 14: Using Social Media   201
  Blogging   203
  Twitter   210
  Facebook   212
  LinkedIn   214
  Video   214

CHAPTER 15: From Farm Shops to Supermarkets   215
  Local retailers   217
  Regional and national retailers   225
  Pitch tips for meeting supermarket buyers   229
  Box schemes and online stores   230

CHAPTER 16: Selling at Events   233
  Farmers' markets   235
  Food festivals   238
  Farmers' market and festival kit list   240
  Running a successful stall   244

Conclusion   257
  Links   258

Index   267

Introduction

Many of us dream of being our own boss, working from home and turning a hobby into money. With a bit of hard work, planning and help, the dream is certainly within reach.

Whether you are in full-time employment and wish to earn a second income or are looking for a complete change of lifestyle, this guide will tell you everything you need to know to start your own food business.

The only thing it doesn't cover is recipes, and that's because it's designed to help people with interests in *every* kind of food: from cupcakes to crabcakes, sausages to salads.

Now is a great time to start your own food business. You'll be tapping into the public's desire for a return to traditional, well-cooked, homemade food. You'll also be able to sell your products at a growing number of local food fairs, farmers' markets and food festivals. Supermarkets, too, are increasingly receptive.

And with modern technology and social media, it's never been easier to promote your products.

Working with food is great fun. Yes, it's demanding. But the rewards can be substantial, both financially and creatively. You don't need to be a Michelin-starred chef to earn money from food. All it takes is the ability to learn fast, work hard and be adaptable.

What this book does

This book will help you:

- ★ turn your love of food into a thriving small business, with the right idea and a watertight business plan

- ★ create a home-based kitchen that complies with health and safety legislation

- ★ use social media to promote your produce and brand cost-effectively

- ★ become part of a vibrant community selling at farmers' markets and food festivals across the UK

- ★ sell into shops, pubs and giant supermarket chains.

This book is sprinkled with real-life stories of people making money from cooking, baking, blogging and much more besides. We'll meet soft drink producers, beef burger and sausage makers, chocolate and fudge specialists – all of whom started from scratch and are now successfully selling into everywhere from farm shops to supermarkets.

"We'll meet soft drink producers, beef burger and sausage makers, chocolate and fudge specialists . . ."

I hope this book will be the recipe you need to become a successful food entrepreneur just like them.

Bruce McMichael

PART
ONE

Starting Your Food Business

CHAPTER 1

Cooking up a Great Idea

STARTING YOUR HOME-BASED FOOD BUSINESS

Take a pinch of optimism, a spoonful of passion and a good measure of hard work and you have the basic ingredients for a home-based food business.

Have you always worked for someone else, but secretly dreamed of being your own boss? Faced with a discouraging job market, perhaps you've thought about creating your own job? Maybe you have a book full of recipes just waiting to get out there.

Whatever your motivation, running your own food business from home is a wonderful opportunity and should, I believe, be grasped with both hands.

It's important to understand what it *isn't*, though.

It isn't merely an expansion of ordinary kitchen life – cooking and baking for family, guests or fun. To an observer, scaling up to commercial production is just a matter of *more* – more ingredients, more measuring, more cooking.

The full picture is not quite so simple.

Creating a profitable business demands investment in time, skills, equipment. Perhaps, too, in facilities and business and technical support. Most of all it requires a different mindset: a shift from producing for your own pleasure to producing for your own profit.

None of this, of course, need be daunting, expensive or soulless – and this book will help you navigate your way through it all. But the difference in approach – really in attitude – does need to be borne in mind from the start.

Running your own food business is more challenging than cooking for fun. Thankfully, it's also a lot more rewarding.

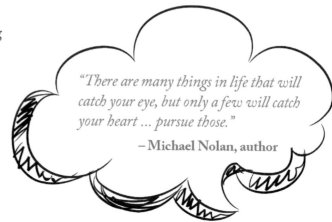

"There are many things in life that will catch your eye, but only a few will catch your heart ... pursue those."

– **Michael Nolan, author**

KEY STEPS IN CREATING YOUR BUSINESS

This is the age of ethnic cooking, gastro pubs and local produce. Provenance, animal welfare and culinary innovation are important as perhaps never before. The British food revolution demands high quality food, backed up with a story and integrity. It also increasingly seeks value. This is the space which a new wave of food entrepreneurs are successfully occupying, and the arena this book is all about helping you to enter.

The route to success today looks something like the following:

* **Research** – is there a market for your product or service?

* **Business plan** – write a plan; a route-map to business success.

* **Get cooking** – deliver food that beats your customers' expectations.

* **Marketing and selling** – use everything from word-of-mouth to websites and social media to share what makes your produce the best.

The rest of this chapter and the next will focus on getting and perfecting your idea through research, with the remainder of the book taking you through the other steps.

WHAT'S YOUR NICHE?

So, do you want to be a cupcake-baker, bread-maker, food stylist or photographer, recipe-writer or wedding-caterer – to create artisan produce or dream up international brands?

There are endless ways you can turn your passion for food into a business.

Start by asking: **what is my niche?** What skills, experience and interests in food do I have, and what marketplace(s) does this lead to?

The right speciality, effectively occupied, will be profitable. And don't feel you have to run away from competitive markets or reinvent the (cheese) wheel. It's okay to do things just slightly differently, maybe just more effectively, than others out there.

What twists of your own can you add?

TIP: Consider Fraser Doherty of Scotland's SuperJam business (*www.superjam.co.uk*). As a fresh-faced 14-year old, Fraser used his grandmother's recipe and his mother's kitchen to enter the overcrowded jam market – standing out by making it healthy and fun. SuperJam is now selling all over the UK and building a strong export market.

The three Cs of the food business

There are three Cs that are key to every successful food business:

Cuisine

Offer food that you're familiar with and can produce at consistently high quality. You want clients that clean their plates and come back for more, and you want to be able to successfully serve them when they do.

Cook

Although you might be a great cook, you mustn't rest on your laurels. A successful food business will require you to challenge yourself and improve all the time. You may also need to hire staff at some stage. This is one of the most difficult and important tasks of a small business owner. Great chefs produce great food. Be prepared to nurture them so you can handle other aspects of the business.

Concept

A focused concept is important. Specialising in a particular service helps potential clients quickly grasp what you offer. It also helps you direct your marketing efforts and build your reputation.

Think in terms of food sources, locations, events, meal types – all filtered through your own talents and interests – and potential combinations of these.

Here's an example of a gourmet catering/private chef business. They started with an interest in hog roasts. This led to the following notes as they worked up their business idea:

Experience: hog roasts

Locations: outdoor, BBQs

Ethnic variations: Southeast Asia, Italian, South American/Peruvian

Events: weddings, anniversaries, birthdays, funerals

Other possibilities: sandwiches for offices, cafés

RESEARCH

"When I walk into my kitchen today, I am not alone. Whether we know it or not, none of us is. We bring fathers and mothers and kitchen tables, and every meal we have ever eaten. Food is never just food. It's also a way of getting at something else: who we are, who we have been, and who we want to be."

– Molly Wizenberg, *A Homemade Life: Stories and Recipes from My Kitchen Table* (2009)

Researching the market to find and test your business ideas is vital. "Just because you cook it, it does not mean that they will come," warns Olga Astaniotis of The Olive Grows, a company offering start-up companies kitchen space and business advice.

"The subjective opinions of your friends and family and even the uniqueness of your product do not necessarily equate to a brilliant business idea that you are equipped to execute."

You will need to make some very smart decisions throughout your business life. Especially in the business's early days. This starts with research.

First steps

Here are ten places to start finding and testing your ideas for a food business.

1. Ask your local deli or farm shop what they would like to see on their shelves.

2. Social media – get on Twitter, Facebook and YouTube and ask people what they're interested in. Upload photos and videos of different food ideas you've had and see which get the warmest response.

3. The media: TV, magazines and newspapers are a good indication of current food trends. Listen to *The Food Programme* on BBC Radio 4, and check out great food bloggers.

4. How can you improve upon existing products? Think in terms of flavour *and* nutrition. Both are big selling points.

5. Attend food networking events, go to food shows, festivals, farmers' markets. Get to know local producers and feed off their enthusiasm.

6. Discover new ingredients in speciality shops and delis.

7. Make a list of everyday food and drink and think about how you could improve on it. Do the same for your favourite meals – both home-cooked and from restaurants.

8. Explore the science of nutrition in a short course.

9. Sign up for advanced-level cookery lessons.

10. Ask family and friends. (And *experiment* on family and friends!)

Networking group More to Life Than Shoes has three research tips for budding foodie entrepreneurs beginning to explore the possibilities out there:

1. Get skilled up

Learn as many new and useful skills as possible. Go on courses – computing, bookkeeping, food safety. Get qualified. Volunteer for a charity or community group in your sector to gain contacts and skills.

2. Embrace the side project

Use time on the train, during lunch, on the bus. Learn as much as you can. Read cookbooks, cookery and lifestyle magazines. Question friends, family, people on farmers' market stalls.

3. Break it down

If you have a job, don't immediately resign. Once you know what you want to do, break it down into smaller steps and take them one at a time. These aren't scary things when you start out small, and they'll make things happen.

★ More to Life Than Shoes | *www.moretolifethanshoes.com*

"You'll need to look after yourself. Catering requires a certain level of fitness to handle the amount of physical work involved: from transporting heavy items to standing on your feet cooking and serving at a dinner or behind a market stall in the cold and rain for hours."

– Henrietta Green of FoodLovers Britain
(*www.foodloversbritain.com*)

You'll know your hobby is ready to become a business when:

* You make your children tell you about their school dinners so you can do a nutritional analysis.

* You have taken to scribbling down brilliant recipe ideas in the middle of the night.

* Your partner is losing sleep and putting on weight.

SOURCE: COUNTRY LIVING MAGAZINE

CASE STUDY
EDIBLE ORNAMENTALS

Joanna Plumb's food business, Edible Ornamentals, has gone from strength to strength after market research provided through IGD helped convince her to make a small but significant change to her strategy.

This case study comes from IGD. IGD provides information, insight and research for the food and grocery industry including conferences with retailers, market research reports, workshops. Joanna started the business while she was at home looking after her young son.

In 2010, Joanna attended an IGD's 'Sell more – waste less' workshop at Newmarket to learn more about the idea of 'value' and how it drives shopper behaviour. In particular Joanna wanted to better understand which products to promote at her farm shop at Cherwood Nursery, Chawston in Bedfordshire. As well as the farm shop the nursery includes a greenhouse and a commercial kitchen where sauces and other gourmet chilli-based products are prepared.

IGD prepared a shopper insight report for Joanna, using information from a Kent Business School survey:

* The weekly sales for chilli sauces fluctuate over the year but it could be seen that sweet chilli sauce sales always peak during January, which coincides with the Chinese New Year.

* Sales of chilli sauces overall had grown 10% in value over the last year, but volume sales remained unchanged. Shoppers had switched from sweet chilli sauces to normal chilli sauces.

* People buying chilli sauces were also likely to buy other types of sauces, such as other oriental sauces and dipping sauces.

"We know what we like, but when we're developing new products to sell to the public, it's important for us to know what the customer actually wants. Having accurate market information that has been properly researched can be invaluable to small companies like us so that we can add exciting new products to our range of sauces that people really will buy, and won't just sit on the shelf," says Joanna.

* Edible Ornamentals | *www.edibleornamentals.co.uk*

* IGD | *www.igd.com*

* Kent Business School | *www.kent.ac.uk/kbs*

Your USP

USP, or unique selling point, describes the one thing that distinguishes your products within a crowded market. It's a touchstone for just about everything to do with you business. Ultimately, it's your voice in the marketplace.

Work out your USP using the following steps and then let your customers know about it.

* Understand **why** a customer would use your product or service. What benefits does it offer them? What do they get out of using your product?

* How might your product or service be positively **different** from your competition?

* **Listen** to your customers! What you consider important may not interest the people buying your food. Look for gaps to see where you can really differentiate from the competition.

TIP: One way of working out your USP is to put together a so-called 'elevator' pitch. Imagine you have just two minutes (the average elevator journey) to describe your business to a potential customer. What would you say?

Finding and keeping your customers

You'll need to research your potential customers, the competition and a price point by visiting competitors' sites, foodie sites and forums, reading reports and seeking intelligence from experts.

Look for information that will answer the following questions:

> *"Who might your customers be? How do they spend their money? Where do they shop?"*

* What is the **number** of potential customers you can serve, and how do these customers like to be served?

* What are their **characteristics**, spending patterns, and who are their key influencers?

* **Who** is currently serving your market?

* **Where** are your potential customers going for their ingredients and food?

* What do they **like** about what they're getting and, more importantly, what do they **dislike** (as this opens up opportunities for you to improve on the status quo)?

In view of the above, is there a business here? Is there room in the market? Is there genuine demand?

CASE STUDY
INNOCENT DRINKS

When three university friends – Adam Balon, Richard Reed and Jon Wright – opened a smoothie stall at a local jazz festival, they asked the music fans to vote on whether or not they should give up their day jobs and sell the drinks full-time.

The response was overwhelmingly positive. After resigning from their jobs the next day, Innocent Drinks was born.

A decade later, Innocent was turning over more than £100m. It is now majority owned by Coca-Cola.

As Innocent's Richard Reed says:

> "What itch are you scratching for your customer? What problem are you solving for them?"

★ Innocent | *www.innocentdrinks.co.uk*

Running the numbers

Statistics can be hard to come by, but there are some key sources offering numbers and data about who's making and who's buying food and drink.

★ **Food Farm reports** | Government gathered food and
  farming statistics can be found here:
  www.defra.gov.uk/statistics/foodfarm

★ *The Food Statistics Pocketbook* | This resource contains
  a wide range of statistics on the production and consumption of
  UK food: *www.defra.gov.uk/statistics/foodfarm/food/pocketstats*

★ **Family Food reports** | These look at levels of consumer purchasing of food and
  drink: *www.defra.gov.uk/statistics/foodfarm/food/familyfood*

★ **Chilled Food Association** | Market data for chilled food from Kantar Worldpanel:
  www.chilledfood.org

★ **Key Note** | Hundreds of free executive summaries of food and drink reports
  published are available at *www.keynote.co.uk*

★ **Mintel Oxygen** | Although you'll have to pay
  for detailed Mintel reports, for basic
  research it is worth reading
  accompanying brochures which
  summarise key findings and statistics:
  www.oxygen.mintel.com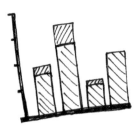

The Food and Drink Federation (FDF)

The Food and Drink Federation (*www.fdf.org.uk*) says it is the voice of the UK food and drink industry, putting the industry's point of view to the government, regulators, consumers and the media.

FDF has dozens of food-producing companies as members. Several industry groups also belong, including the Association of Bakery Ingredient Manufacturers; the British Coffee Association; and the UK Herbal Infusions Association.

For small and medium-sized companies, the FDF offers support ranging from technical to networking groups.

CHAPTER 2

Types of Food Business

There are two basic types of home-based food business: caterers and suppliers. A business, of course, needn't be confined to one or the other. Though it often works out that way for efficiency's sake, don't be afraid to experiment – each has a lot to teach the other.

Caterers, for instance, always do better for making sure their branding is as memorable and consistent as suppliers'. And suppliers who are forthcoming with delicious samples and live cooking demonstrations tend to rake in more contracts and punters.

CATERING

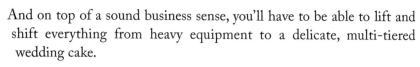

What is a caterer?

Catering is the business of providing food at a site such as a hotel, pub, sports ground or other location. A *mobile* caterer serves food directly from a vehicle or cart at outdoor events ranging from music festivals to county shows, as well as at offices and food festivals.

As a caterer, you'll need to wear many different hats. You'll need a good understanding of cooking and serving on a commercial scale. You'll have to be a competent planner, a great marketeer and inspiring salesperson.

And on top of a sound business sense, you'll have to be able to lift and shift everything from heavy equipment to a delicate, multi-tiered wedding cake.

There'll also be lots of cleaning of pots and pans.

Why choose catering?

Countless food and drink companies start up each year in the UK. While many do not make it past their first anniversary, the success rate of catering businesses is high, thanks to lower overheads and reduced staff costs – employees are only needed for planned events, and mobile catering businesses can be run part-time.

Special considerations

* With clients seeking catering for events such as weddings, funerals and Christenings, you may find yourself getting involved in the planning of the event itself. This type of work suits organised people with culinary and organisational flair. However, planning such events is time-consuming and can be stressful, with clients hoping for the 'perfect day'.

* Marketing is often word-of-mouth, so you'll need to be personable.

* Serving food in corporate situations – in boardrooms, say, or at a conference – is a competitive market, with many contracts already served by local restaurants. But it pays well. While business clients need feeding all year, their tastes and demands may limit the range of food you provide.

* At many large events, existing caterers already have exclusive contracts with the organisers and jealously guard their rights. Pick your events carefully and don't be surprised if you're bumped off the list at the last minute. Some organisers will allow

multiple vendors, others not. This is less of a problem at farmers' markets and other similar events, where organisers will allow two or three similar stalls.

★ Industrial catering is where you provide large volumes of food, for example to schools, airlines and other institutions. It's unlikely that your business will start at industrial scale, but you may grow or sell into such a company.

Research for outdoor catering companies

If you are planning to open an outdoor catering company, your customers will expect to have a certain amount of background material about your business and the food you'll be serving. Questions will normally be based around the following:

★ *Flexibility*: How flexible is your menu; how much freedom do clients have in deciding the menu?

★ *Taste and sampling*: Can clients taste your food before making a decision?

★ *Menu*: Do you cater for special diets – gluten-free, vegetarian, etc.? Does the price include starter, main course and dessert? What about tea, coffee and *petits fours*?

★ *Seasonality*: If you are negotiating to cater an event planned for the summer or autumn, think about food available at the time.

★ *Buffet or sit-down dinner*: Do you specialise in catering buffets or full meals? Can you provide late-night buffets, for example at a wedding?

★ *References*: Can potential clients speak to your existing clients? Choose carefully who you would recommend as references. Ask them permission to use their name.

* *Full service*: Do you provide linens, tables, chairs, flowers and decoration? Is this open to negotiation? Perhaps you can hire in furniture on request. Can you provide audio-visual equipment? Do you provide service staff?

* *Your kitchen*: If your client wishes to meet you at your home, are you prepared for this? You'll need a place to meet, and a clean and tidy working area.

* *Organisation*: Your client will expect you to be very organised and efficient. If you are delivering a quote, do so within the time agreed.

* *Small print*: Be very clear about what is included in your quote and service. Answer questions such as: is corkage included; who tips the serving staff; is there a deadline for increasing or cutting back on numbers of guests?

* *Discounts*: Potential clients will often ask for discounts. Off-peak times may include mid-week weddings, quiet months, e.g. January and February. Be prepared to negotiate. Have a clear idea of your margins and ensure that the event will result in a profit.

TIP: Take photographs of your work to show prospective clients how you design platters of food, tables and serve the food and drink.

PRODUCER

Selling at farmers' markets, local shops, restaurants, and directly to customers

What is a producer?

Many people start their home-based food business by becoming a producer. Whether making cupcakes or loose-leaf tea, you source, create and brand your own food products and sell them onto customers – as a supplier to (for example) restaurants or as a direct seller to individuals.

Choosing the right product for your target market is key here. You'll need to keep on top of fast-moving trends and ensure your product range keeps up-to-date with customers' desires.

People often get the motivation for supplying or selling their own food products after being praised for making a delicious dish at home. This can be a good starting point, but remember to do your market research and make sure there's enough profit in it for you. Restaurants and shops will need to add their own margin to your products – do your numbers have room for this? (More on this in chapters 3 and 4.)

Why choose producing?

It's incredibly rewarding to see your products on the shelves of a shop or on a restaurant menu. And it's even nicer receiving compliments from customers at a farmers' market or festival, knowing that what you have made has brightened people's meals up. Supplying and selling your own brand of food is a well-trod path to kitchen dominance: everyone from Green & Blacks to Levi Roots of Reggae Reggae Sauce has navigated it.

Being a producer also involves a little less 'live' stress than catering. When it's showtime – a pitch to a pub chain, say, or selling to punters at a food fair – your products are already finished and ready to taste. You know they're delicious, and in that respect, at least, nothing can go wrong on the day: nothing can get burnt, or spilt, or fail to come together as you wanted.

Special considerations

At the same time, pitching to other businesses and running your own stalls or shop will involve stresses of their own kind. You'll need to have mastered the numbers and be on top of them at all times. You'll need to be able to negotiate. And you'll need to be able to make others fall in love with your products more than your rivals'.

* You will need a passion for your chosen market niche, as your waking hours will be spent thinking about the business, preparing the food to sell, preparing to attend food festivals and enthusing everyone you meet about your food.

* You'll need to keep a close watch on your expenses and income to make sure the business isn't wasting money. Overproducing and underselling is a danger that must be constantly watched for. Also, factor in the cost of exhibiting.

* It's vital that you test your products with your potential market before investing lots of time and money. Get a neutral opinion from the marketplace, and the views of traders already active in your sector.

★ Do you have the support of friends and family members? Your cooking and food preparation will take up a lot of space and time in your home kitchen. Are they prepared for the inevitable disruption of family life? (Are you?) Also, you may need to call upon their time (unpaid) to help you at a farmers' market, early in the morning on a cold Sunday in January.

Hampers

One of the many routes-to-market for a producer is hampers. If you create the right product, you can get it included in a hamper sold by a local hamper company or regional food body.

Case Study

WENLOCK HAMPERS

Wenlock Hampers were initially created to tie in with the London Olympic Games and their historical links with the small town of Much Wenlock in Shropshire. A popular Wenlock Hamper is an assortment of food and drink products made within a 26.2-mile radius of Much Wenlock – a marathon's distance!

Products in the hampers include cheese, chutney, meats, infused rapeseed oil, chocolate, beer and wine. All products are selected from HEFF-producer members, and made in compliance with the HEFF Standard, a health and hygiene third party audit.

★ HEFF | *www.heff.co.uk*

CHAPTER 3

Refining Your Ideas

H opefully the first two chapters have given you plenty of food for thought. Is your kitchen notepad starting to fill up with notes and ideas? Great – because now it's time to start refining your business and product ideas.

"You don't have to cook fancy or complicated masterpieces – just good food from fresh ingredients."

— Julia Child, American cook and author (1912–2004)

FOCUS GROUPS

Gather a group of friends and family and share your ideas with them – if possible with samples. Try to also do this with five or six people who represent your target market. People are usually happy to eat a bit of free food in return for their thoughts.

Have question sheets prepared in advance – anonymised if you think it will help honesty. And you do want people to be **brutally honest**.

Encourage your focus groups to contribute as many suggestions as possible when discussing your ideas. Ask for normal *and* zany contributions. It will all help – you never know what inspiration it might spark.

Don't be afraid to fail

Survival of the fittest is not based on strength but adaptability. When working through your ideas you need to base your thinking on why the business could work, not why it could fail. If you don't try something out of fear, you'll never know whether it would have been a success or not. Just be prepared to adapt.

Get help from food groups

Ask your local or regional food group for help. Deliciously Yorkshire, which covers Humberside as well as Yorkshire, says:

> "It is easy to become too close to your products and not see the potential or what is stopping them being a success. We hold regular focus groups where you can submit one or more of your products for consumer panel feedback."

★ Deliciously Yorkshire | *www.deliciouslyorkshire.co.uk*

Trend-watching

Trend-watching is a really important technique for any food business, especially at this stage. Trend-watching helps you deliver products and services to markets that are currently proving profitable. It can also provide you with ideas for products based on what has worked already in other countries.

For instance, China is arguably the fastest-growing consumer market in the world. This fact is not lost on London's luxury department store, Harrods, which now employs several

Mandarin-speaking staff. So, if you're selling luxury puddings or drinks, consider having labels printed in both English and Mandarin.

Here's a selection of food businesses reported on trend-watching site *springwise.com* to inspire your thoughts. Some maybe too *avant garde* or not relevant to your thinking, but they have a common theme: engaging with customers in new, innovative ways builds brand loyalty and sales.

Solar-powered pop-ups

Finland's Lapin Kulta Solar Kitchen Restaurant is a pop-up venture using only the energy of the sun to cook food. The restaurant opens only on sunny days, and its offerings depend on how much sunshine is available at the time of cooking, ranging from full solar barbecues to lower-temperature meals and salads.

★ *www.lapinkultasolarkitchenrestaurant.com*

Food of friends

Food giant Heinz in the UK used Facebook as a platform for fans to send personalised tins of soup to friends suffering with a cold.

★ *www.facebook.com/HeinzSoupUK*

Home-made kits

In Alberta, Canada, Make Cheese enables households to produce their own cheese, with all-in-one kits containing ingredients, equipment and recipes. Providing consumers with simple ways to create their own produce in the home, initiatives such as these offer chemical-free and cheaper alternatives to supermarket shopping.

★ *www.makecheese.ca*

Foodie trend-watching on Twitter

★ @trendwatching   ★ @springwise   ★ @psfk

★ @kickstarter   ★ @coolhunter

Avoiding useless USPs

When fixing on your business's unique selling point, it's easy to prioritise *unique* over *selling*. The current trend for chilli sauces provides a cautionary tale.

"One of the most common product ideas bought to our kitchens is chilli sauce," says food consultant Olga Astaniotis of The Olive Grows. The prospective entrepreneur invariably claims their product is "not just any chilli sauce, but made with chillies from a specific region, using a specific mix of chillies *and* a secret ingredient from their ancestors, with a unique flavour like no other on the market.

"Whilst this is valid differentiation from competition, the question must be asked and answered honestly: does the consumer care enough about these differentiating factors? Deciding that they are a USP and their truly being a USP are two very different things."

Shelves in delis, farmers' markets and supermarkets are groaning with colourful displays of chilli sauce. You must remember customer behaviour, and what actually drives purchases of different products. For chilli sauces, says Olga, it's actually "pricing and branding" not "unique flavour or piquancy".

> "Those that succeed in food businesses understand customers' needs and how they want those needs fulfilled."

★ Olga Astaniotis, The Olive Grows | *www.theolivegrows.org*

Having your cake

Cake businesses have flourished in the wake of TV programmes like the BBC's *Great British Bake Off*. Insurance broker Simply Business (*www.simplybusiness.co.uk*) recorded:

★ a 54% increase in cake-making businesses in 2011

★ a 325% increase in cake-making businesses since 2009

In fact, baking cakes has risen to become the eighteenth most popular start-up business idea in Britain today. Over 90% of these businesses are run by women. But the number of male bakers is also growing. The majority of cake businesses are started by those in their 20s and 30s, with almost half of those starting a cake business falling between the ages of 25 and 34, and a third between 35 and 44.

TIP: Local partnerships can help reach potential customers. Team up with local wedding and birthday venues to offer discounted cakes to their customers. Partner with other local businesses such as florists, delicatessens and gift shops to pool your customer bases by recommending each other's complementary services.

CASE STUDY
LET IT BE CAKE

Elsa Santana, aged 34, set up her cake-making business, Let it Be Cake, in August 2011 after leaving her career in IT to start a family.

"I'd been baking cakes for friends and family for years," says Elsa. "Eventually I decided to take the plunge and launched Let it Be Cake as a proper business. Recent TV shows like *Cake Boss* and *The Great British Bake Off* definitely acted as an inspiration and catalyst for my business plan – making me realise that there was a real appetite out there for bespoke cakes like mine."

"Cake-making offers an appealing business model, especially to mums like me. It allows you to work from home in a very creative industry and to control the hours you work.

"It's very rewarding. Seeing the appreciation on your client's face makes long hours of fiddly cake decoration worthwhile!"

TIP: "Cake-makers tend to have a very local customer base, so even though there is lots of competition out there, you can carve a niche in your area."

★ Let it Be Cake | *www.letitbecake.co.uk*

Four-legged customers

Why should we humans get all the best food? What about starting a gourmet dog food business? You'll still need to be adept in food preparation, baking and cooking. But rather than producing cupcakes and cookies for kids, you could be making dry pet food, cookies and treats for dogs and cats.

Pet fairs and many farmers' markets will welcome your presence. You can also make sales into pet stores and chains. Owners are willing to pay a premium to get high quality, healthy food for their animals, and pet food typically offers high profit margins – particularly if made (and sold) the right way.

Says one home-based dog food manufacturer:

> "I use natural chicken broth in my treats. I think if you're making a chicken-flavoured treat it should have chicken in it. Why put an artificial chemical flavouring in it when you can use the real thing?"

One rather unique pet-food business is BeuteFuchs of Munich, Germany, a store that creates custom organic diets for its customers' dogs.

BeuteFuchs sources organic meat from across Germany (everything from lamb to duck and goose in season) and provides such delicacies for discerning pet-owners as organic grain-free muscle meat with a vegetable fruit mix and high quality oil.

> "Their USP? Not simply delicious food, but meals that result in better pet health, lower veterinary bills and less excrement."

Their USP? Not simply delicious food, but meals that result in better pet health, lower veterinary bills and less excrement.

TIP: Big 'nos' for any dog recipes include grapes, onions, raisins and macadamia nuts. It's vital to check with your vet for a full list of do's and don'ts.

★ BeuteFuchs | *www.beutefuchs.de*

COOKING SCHOOLS

Cooking schools can help you develop your skills, get advice from professionals, expand your horizons into new cuisines and markets, and build your contacts. All valuable at every stage of running a food business, but particularly when refining your initial ideas.

If you decide to go on a course, there are some issues you'll need to consider:

Tutors

What's the ratio of teacher to pupils? Do you prefer one-to-one tuition, or groups? You might benefit in groups from questions being asked by fellow students.

Facilities

Newer schools will probably have state-of-the-art equipment. Alternatively, learning in an older pub or restaurant kitchen means you might get a better feeling for true commercial catering.

Some schools sell themselves on having Agas – would this be relevant to you? For example, Eckington Manor Cookery School in Worcestershire uses Agas and Falcon Range cookers and has accommodation on site.

Cost

Be very clear what you expect to learn from the course, and how it will benefit your business. As the cost of attending is directly related to your business, it will be a business expense.

UK and Irish cookery schools and resources

Cookery schools

★ Ashburton Cookery School | *www.ashburtoncookeryschool.co.uk*

Caters for domestic cooks and offers a six-month professional chef training programme.

★ The School of Artisan Food | *www.schoolofartisanfood.org*

Offers courses to suit all skill levels, expanding knowledge through a wide range of short courses, and a one-year Advanced Diploma in either butchery and charcuterie, baking or dairy.

* Brompton Cookery School | *www.bromptoncookeryschool.co.uk*

Based on a National Trust property near Shrewsbury, Shropshire.

* Eckington Manor Cookery School | *www.eckingtonmanorcookeryschool.co.uk*

Based in Worcestershire, it offers a week-long professional chef course covering staffing to menu planning.

* Le Cordon Bleu | *www.cordonbleu.net*

Famous school based in central London, offers courses lasting from one day to 12 months.

* Leiths | *www.leiths.com*

Based in West London, this famous cookery school teaches creative cooking classes, from cookery diplomas to one-day, evening and one-week cooking courses.

* Billingsgate Seafood Training School | *www.seafoodtraining.org*

Set up as a charity, this school offers training to people coming into the seafood industry or who want to improve their understanding of it.

* Cordon Vert | *www.cordonvert.co.uk*

Offers professional courses for those interested in vegetarian cookery.

* Fat Hen | *www.fathen.org*

Prepare and cook foraged foods at this Cornish cookery school.

* The Empire Farm | *www.empirefarm.co.uk*

This Somerset-based, organic farm is the venue for a wide range of butchery and smallholder courses.

Resources

* Next Step | *nextstep.direct.gov.uk*

Government-supported reference site with advice on courses, careers, redundancy and funding.

* Hot Courses | *www.hotcourses.com*

Lists over a million courses offered in the UK, with reviews.

* Floodlight | *london.floodlight.co.uk*

Courses and colleges in London and increasingly elsewhere.

* City & Guilds | *www.cityandguilds.com*

A leading vocational awarding body providing courses and qualifications.

* The Open University | *www.open-university.co.uk*

University-standard food courses including food-science skills, preservation and packaging. General business courses also available.

CHAPTER 4

Planning Your Business

S o, you've got a great idea for a new food company. After the initial flush of excitement, it's time to get your business going.

How do you turn your passion into a profit-making machine? It's all in the planning. The next two chapters will explain the ins and outs: from putting together a business plan to working out costs and getting funding.

BUSINESS PLAN

Many people dread working on business plans. There's really no need to feel anxious. It can be a simple, logical process. And an effective, *realistic* business plan will pay dividends throughout the life of a business.

Business plans are there to help keep your objectives in view. They're there to keep problems in perspective. And they're there to reignite passion whenever motivation flags or difficulties arise. They are a roadmap for your business.

Some are written on the backs of envelopes, others are pages long and bound in beautiful folders. However they are presented, they must fulfil the same job. They must communicate your business goals and the basic processes you will follow to meet them.

You can use the following broad headings to organise your business plan:

* **Idea** – what is your product or service?

* **Market** – who are your customers?

* **Operations** – how will you produce and deliver your offer?

* **Financials** – what are your costs, how much will you charge for the finished product, and does this show a profit? (The answer needs to be yes!)

* **Friends** – do you have a support network of advisors in place?

Whether you're approaching your bank manager, an investment angel or working out a strategy for growth, a business plan is a vital document. And if there is one lesson we should all take from watching the business pitches rolled out on *Dragons' Den*, it's **know your figures**.

TIP: Be sure to build your business on what your customers need and want, not what you think they want. If they don't want what you're selling and you can't create a need, then the business will struggle.

CASE STUDY

FOODLOVERS BRITAIN

In the early 1990s, Henrietta Green, food writer and farmers' market enthusiast, met an ex-coal miner in the north of England making and selling chocolate products from his garage.

The chocolate was delicious and a great example of a passion being realised in an unexpected location, says Henrietta, who now runs *www.foodloversbritain.com* and is a pioneering force in the current farmers' market movement.

The FoodLovers Britain website runs an approval system and online shop, highlighting the huge changes that enable producers to sell their goods online. Today the route to market for small food businesses must include the internet – it's just as important for them as it is for supermarkets.

In Henrietta's experience, the secret of a successful business is a well-planned business.

"More people are setting up from home without fully appreciating the range of skills they will need to create a profitable and sustainable business," she says.

"If your business plan is in your head, it's not a business plan. Write it down." And don't be shy about making sure you'll be profitable. "You may be turning out lots of lovely products or providing a great service – but are you making a profit?"

★ FoodLovers Britain | *www.foodloversbritain.com*

FINANCIALS

For a food business, margins can be tight and costs can escalate quickly. Getting financials right is particularly important. Here's some more detail on the key points that must be covered by a food-based business plan and its financial section.

Summary of financial needs

How much money will you need to run the business for the first year, bearing in mind you'll need to include living expenses for you (and perhaps your family)?

Do you need to raise money? If so, include the loan repayments in this section. Do you need to buy or rent equipment? Build a website? It all goes in here.

Sales forecast

If you are setting up an outside catering company, estimate how many jobs you will get on a monthly basis for at least the first 12 months of trading.

If you sell at farmers' markets and through local shops, estimate sales on a per-event basis. Be conservative with your estimates.

Catering can be a seasonal business; wedding caterers will probably find the spring and summer periods busy, with business slowing towards November and December. But chocolatiers may find the reverse. Factor this in, and consider how you will pay your bills in your quiet months.

Profit margins

In the early days, food costs will be probably be relatively high. Things go wrong. Mistakes happen. You might not have the economies of scale yet. And if you're a caterer, events may not pan out as you anticipated.

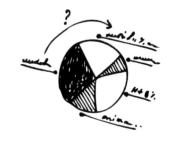

As you gain experience, you'll improve at ordering the right amount of food. Decreasing wastage will mean costs falling over time. Recognise this in your financial plan. Your biggest *variable* cost as a caterer will probably be labour, so if you will need to hire help, factor this in as well.

Cash flow forecast

Like any business, tracking of costs and control of cash flow is vital. Before you get paid for a job or product, you'll have invested a certain amount of money (and time) in getting it completed. If you haven't the cash to meet those costs, even though you might be able to record a theoretical profit, you'll be in trouble – staff, suppliers and landlords might need to get paid long before your customer pays you. And by the time you are paid there may not be much of a business left.

Properly managed cash flow ensures that enough cash is kept on hand to meet such predictable – as well as some unpredictable – expenses. It goes hand in hand with making sure that payment terms for your customers are clear; and, if possible, negotiated to be prompt (perhaps with a mild discount incentive for early payment).

It also involves getting the most generous possible payment terms from *your* suppliers.

Capital spending plan

Capital spending means investing in things like equipment – from refrigerated vans to ovens and freezers. Leasing large items like this can reduce high costs at the start of the business. Credit is not always available to new businesses, though.

Price and pricing

New businesses often underprice their products. And whilst value is indeed vital, prioritising cheapness is unwise for a small food business.

Firstly, people looking for the cheapest product will not be good long-term customers. Secondly, rival companies also prioritising cheapness will either be sufficiently enormous and deep-pocketed as to render competition (on price alone) pointless, or will be small businesses cutting corners on quality or taking a loss. The latter won't be around for long. In truth, there's little point worrying about either.

To ensure you're pricing your goods fairly, you need to know your costs. Whatever the unit cost, a rough rule of thumb is to charge four or five times this as the purchase price. (Though be careful: this is just a rule of thumb. Check out Chapter 5 for more detail on how to get it right for each product-type.)

It's vital that the value of your product is conveyed in line with the price you are charging. Food consultant Rob Ward of *www.foodmarketingnetwork.com* says customers moan when they feel they are not getting value for money – not necessarily when things are expensive. The problem is a mismatch between expectations set by a product's price and the experience it actually offers. Ensure that you line this up by positioning your offerings accordingly.

"Look at cars. There are thousands of different models at thousands of different prices. But they all represent value for money to their owners. It must be the same with food."

– Rob Ward, Food Marketing Network

CASE STUDY
SHREWSBURY BAKEHOUSE

American construction project manager Sheila Sager found herself relocating to England with her husband and children in the early 2000s. Fulfilling a long-held ambition of graduating from Oxford University, she then looked around for a business idea as her children reached their late teens and early 20s. Friends suggested following her love of cooking. Maybe she could take her baking skills to the next level?

With this in mind, Sheila talked with local pubs, hotels and restaurants to see whether she might use their kitchens to bake when they were closed. Many of the kitchens were surprisingly small, with no spare place to store equipment, flour or other ingredients.

Sheila realised she needed to try another route. A number of ideas were floated – including converting an old burger van and parking it in the garden. Then a friend volunteered her kitchen. Baking early in the morning and late at night, operating around someone else's family life, worked well for around 18 months. Then the business – Shrewsbury Bakehouse – outgrew the domestic kitchen; and the search for a commercial, town-centre premises began.

A few years later, Sheila now runs Shrewsbury Bakehouse in the heart of Shrewsbury itself. Meanwhile her daughter has been inspired to open a coffee house just two doors away.

Shelia's top start-up observations

Work hard at creating space for your business. Consider having a catering caravan in the garden to free up kitchen space, or converting part of your garage. We used a friend's kitchen to launch the business. Problems we encountered included unsocial hours and everything in the house gradually getting covered in a thin layer of flour.

Keep potential customers in the loop about what you're producing and developing. Get chefs to test your products as they are developed.

Build informal relationships with three or four potential clients. Make sure they are of the quality you want to sell to in the long term. Even if they say no to buying from you at first, you can come away with valuable knowledge. One of our testers noted that our crusts were better on the Saturday – what did we do differently, and could we do that all the time?

Consider your delivery days and dates. Most people do a weekly food shop on Friday or Saturday.

Barter. One pub got free bread for four months in exchange for having our logo on their menu. The landlord recommended us to the pub's customers, helping us build our brand and open doors. Your success is also their success, and we needed their feedback.

Understand different buying philosophies. One customer did not want to take extra product from us despite selling out each week. We didn't understand their buying policy but kept in touch. We didn't take it personally, but kept the relationship warm in the hope that opportunities would arise in future.

Hire for what you need now, not for what you might need in the future. And when using professionals, go for small, local firms rather than large ones. You can always hire larger companies when your turnover and profits justify it and the workload demands it.

Home-makers already possess a huge range of expertise. Don't underestimate skills you might have acquired in organising and running a home. Whether it's managing household budgets, scheduling school runs, gym and dance classes, or negotiating skills acquired from discussions with partners, children and other children's parents – it's all valuable!

If others have a stake in your business, set up a shareholders' agreement before you start. Ensure everyone knows what is expected of them. Set clear roles and targets.

Be clear on how change will be managed – for example, should one business partner want to leave. **" "**

* Shrewsbury Bakehouse | *www.shrewsburybakehouse.co.uk*
* Shrewsbury Coffeehouse | *www.facebook.com/ShrewsburyCoffeehouse*

Finally, be prepared

A business plan should really help you be ready for the future, come what may. Ask yourself – has my plan prepared for the inevitable challenges, such as:

* How will the business handle the loss of a major client or the arrival of a new competitor?

* If finance is not available, what could be sold to cover any shortfall – assets, under-utilised equipment, unwanted stock? Could you delay new product development, mothball new projects?

* What will happen if there are changes in the economy? Have you borrowed, and are you reliant on low interest rates? Have you considered capacity for ramping up production if demand rises – or cutting it back if the economy falters? Will your margins hold up over time?

Business plan advice online

"Brilliant business plans cannot keep a bad caterer in busines."

* Business Link | *www.businesslink.gov.uk*

* Enterprise Nation | *www.enterprisenation.com*

* Smarta | *www.smarta.com*

* HM Revenue & Customs | *www.hmrc.gov.uk*

MENTORS

Having a mentor – an experienced person to look over your business ideas, plans and operations – is extremely valuable. An ideal mentor is someone who comes to the table with:

1. experience of your sector

2. the ability to listen

3. the technical skills to advise

4. a willingness to make introductions to useful contacts.

If there is someone you feel might help, just ask – you'd be surprised who'll say yes. And go for as many as you feel you need: the more perspectives you have, the better.

TIP: You might find your local university or college has a 'business incubator' with staff or contacts able to help you with mentoring. Often your local Chambers of Commerce or Economic Development Board will also be able to assist. Check the Mentorsme site (*www.mentorsme.co.uk*) or see what Horsesmouth (*www.horsesmouth.co.uk*) can offer as well. Other useful websites include *www.rockstargroup.co.uk* and *www.shesingenious.org*.

CASE STUDY
ANGELIC GLUTEN FREE

After graduating from Glasgow's Strathclyde University, Kirsty Gillies began training to become a chartered accountant with a major firm, but quickly realised that her true dream was to create her own food business.

As someone with a gluten intolerance, she identified a gap in the market for quality gluten-free, reduced-fat cookies and biscuits.

Despite her accountancy training, Kirsty admits, one of the hardest tasks in setting up the business was dealing with the numbers – for example, developing budgets and managing cash flow. Studying corporate accountancy is very different from working on the other side of the divide.

With help from her mother, including the use of her kitchen, Kirsty road-tested over 200 recipes for her gluten-free products.

She ruled out outsourcing production in the early days as costs were prohibitive. And, particularly in the early stages, she wanted to retain a hands-on approach.

The longer-term aim, however, is to develop a scaleable business: a brand of cookies with distribution to national markets, and not simply a home-based business making cookies.

"Although manufactured in our kitchen, it's the quality we stress: that's our brand."

Kirsty received start-up support from:

* **Shell LiveWIRE** | "Inspirational and motivational. Great programme of speakers. Good for networking with peers."

* **Prince's Trust** | "Strategic assistance. Helped me clarify the direction of my business, offered funding advice, how to realign my business model, and gave me targets."

TIP: "At the beginning, I spent a lot of time working on the business plan. And now it's checked regularly and undergoes frequent revisions and updates. It's useful for me to keep tabs on how the company is progressing, but it's also a great tool to use when talking with bank managers and seeking funds. A comprehensive business plan gives people confidence in what Angelic Cakes is doing and where we're heading. It shows that we take our business seriously."

* Angelic Gluten Free | *www.angelicglutenfree.co.uk*

CHAPTER 5

Costs and Funding

COSTS

S etting up your business will require spending money on capital equipment (freestanding mixers, food processors, blenders, portable slicers, portable convection oven ...) and variable costs (ingredients).

If you're starting small, you'll probably have much of the equipment you need in your kitchen already. It may not be anything more than ladles, measuring jars, pans, knives, wooden spoons, weighing scales and so on.

If you're looking for a special piece of kit, check out eBay (of course) and places like *Country Living* and *Caterer and Hotelkeeper* magazine. Become a regular customer and friendly face at your local cook-shop. Perhaps you'll be able to negotiate.

* *Good Housekeeping* | *www.goodhousekeeping.co.uk*

* Squires Kitchen | *www.squires-shop.com*

* Cake Craft World | *www.cakecraftworld.co.uk*

* Cake Craft Shop | *www.cakecraftshop.co.uk*

* *Caterer and Hotelkeeper* | *www.caterersearch.com*

* eBay | *www.ebay.co.uk*

Vintage items can also be picked up at charity shops, auctions and car-boot sales. These might come in handy as props for market stalls or in photos that illustrate your products online.

A Country Markets cook's list

What do the pros say? Country Markets suggest that a start-up kitchen will need a selection of the following equipment.

* ★ Food mixer and/or food processor

* ★ Mixing bowls

* ★ Accurate oven

* ★ Silicone sheets: saves time and product wastage

* ★ Oven tins and trays

* ★ Accurate scales. If you can afford trade scales, these are to be recommended: they can be purchased second-hand and recalibrated.

* ★ Food thermometer for oven and fridge. These are handy to confirm the accuracy of your built-in oven and fridge thermometers.

* ★ Stackable cooling wires

* ★ Refractometer: to measure sugar content when making sugar preserves for selling through retail outlets

* ★ Cleaning materials such as antibacterial spray, disposable dishcloths, cotton tea towels and paper towels

* Space. You will need to have somewhere to store extra equipment, packaging material and ingredients, and possibly some product stocks such as preserves, which are often made in large batches.

The experience of Country Markets is that some of these are essential, whilst others are useful to have when the time is right for you. Investing in an extra set of tins and cooling wires, for example, can be a sound investment – but only when orders really starting coming in.

For most people with an interest in cooking, the equipment in their kitchen suits well when starting out. Country Markets Cooks often say that you "just need more of everything" once you are up and running.

* Country Markets | *www.country-markets.co.uk*

From home to business production

Storage

The need for storage multiplies. You'll almost certainly have to set aside space in a garage, utility room or other suitable area for bulk storage. Free-standing shelving can prove vital as a cheap, versatile storage unit.

Timing

Speed becomes extremely important. Thankfully it also naturally increases with practice. Commercial-standard vegetable cutters, slicers and choppers can help high volume throughput if really needed. A commercial-standard food processor may be expensive, but they are robust, flexible and will save time and money in the long term.

Cutlery conundrum

If you're running a catering business, do you need reusable plates, cutlery, crockery and glasses? Don't get caught out unawares. What about salt and pepper pots, tabletop signs (for weddings), table cloths and napkins?

Food safety

Disposable gloves, hairnets, thermometers and a first-aid kit will be needed to meet environmental and health and safety needs. (More on health and safety Chapter 8.)

TIP: If you feel the need to buy new equipment, check that it fulfils these three key requirements: will the business profit more from using this piece of kit than buying something else (advertising, PR, attending a trade show), or keeping the cash for a future need? Secondly, does it meet your long-term business plans? Finally, will the equipment improve product quality? It must also meet safety and regulatory demands.

Negotiating

In the early days of buying ingredients, it's unlikely that you'll be able to negotiate discounts. Get to know your suppliers and warm them up for offering discounts in the future. Large volume purchases attract discounts.

Save in your kitchen

If you can reduce the time taken to gather ingredients and prepare food, your labour costs will be reduced. Identify the key skills you will need and consider taking a catering course to enhance your knowledge (see pages 41–3).

Butchery

If you are working with meat, butchering, cutting, trimming and deboning whole birds, whole fish, and larger cuts of meat, learn how to handle them. If you want smoked food, it can be simple to set up a home-smoker.

★ Meat and Livestock Commercial Services | *www.mlcsl.co.uk*
  Trade body with lots of useful information

★ For Food Smokers | *www.forfoodsmokers.co.uk*
  Home-based smoking advice and equipment

Hate waste

The more you know about how to maximise food use and minimise waste, the more profitable you'll be. Don't over-peel fruits and vegetables; consider cheaper cuts of meat for stews and soups; and use all the bits from fish, meat, or vegetables to make stocks, purées and dips which can be frozen for use later on.

★ Love Food Hate Waste | *www.lovefoodhatewaste.com*
  *Hundreds of recipes and tips about saving food, reducing waste and
  storage*

Manage portion sizes

If you're running a catering company, be consistent and restrained with portion sizes. Bear in mind that if your product is commonly sold in packs of six, or as a quarter pound, then that's what customers will expect and they might be reluctant to pay extra for a different-sized portion, even if it represents better value.

"At one time we were making 5oz burgers, but research showed us that people thought of burgers as being quarter pounders and weren't even aware of the extra ounce of meat in our burgers. We were giving away 20% of the burger unnecessarily."

– Miranda Ballard, Muddy Boots Foods (*www.muddybootsfoods.co.uk*)

Hiring staff

Hiring staff is one of the most stressful parts of running a business. But if you work hard at being a good manager, your staff should be loyal and provide good service.

Your business is your passion, so you can't expect your staff to automatically share the same enthusiasm. Spread it by personally training your staff and telling them as much as you can about the ingredients used and their provenance.

Anyone working for you is an ambassador for your company, representing your brand. They'll need to look clean and neat, be bright and cheerful, reliable and happy to speak to customers and clients. If they are making deliveries to farm shops or delis, occasionally check with the outlets that the service is up to the high standards you expect.

Where to find good staff

1. Acting schools (trainee actors are great front-of-house)
2. Friends and family – maybe they'll volunteer!
3. Students from the local catering college
4. Sixth-form and college students
5. People seeking evening or weekend work
6. Other caterers or local cafés
7. Stay-at-home parents
8. Local job centres

Pay

You must pay your employees and workers at least the national minimum wage and ensure equal pay for men and women. In the very early days of the company, people may be happy to work for some of your produce.

Check out Business Link for advice and guidance on hiring temporary or permanent staff: *www.businesslink.gov.uk/employment*

PRICING

Quoting a price, or range of prices, is one of the most important business jobs you will have.

Margin and mark-up

The terms *margin* and *mark-up* are often confused. Both offer different ways to measure the retailer's share of the price the shopper pays.

Mark-up is the difference as a percentage of the price the retailer charges their customer. Smaller retailers tend to use this approach: they will generally have a percentage mark-up figure in mind for the products they sell.

Many local food producers instead refer to price in terms of margin, which is cost plus profit.

> "Margin and mark-up are often confused. Both offer different ways to measure the retailer's share of the price the shopper pays."

With a bit of simple maths, it's easy to differentiate the two terms. If a product you sell to a retailer at 80p is sold to shoppers at £1, the gross margin is 20% (£1 - 80p as a percentage of £1) and the mark-up is 25% (£1 - 80p as a percentage of 80p).

Getting it right

How do you get your margin/mark-up right? It's best if you tailor it to the market – even when dealing with the same product.

If, for example, you are selling cheese, you may achieve a greater mark-up if it's pitched for display in the 'posher' deli counter rather than the dairy section alongside milk and cream. If your product is spices or herbs, you may be better off charging different prices to natural food stores than delis or larger stores.

Specialist products, such as soft fruit, which don't have a long shelf life may have even higher mark-ups to compensate for such losses. Few shoppers want to buy blemished produce, and shops will throw out food that looks less than fresh.

In fact, such a large percentage of produce purchased by grocery stores is sent to landfill before it reaches the shelves due to spoilage, that retailers typically charge a 50% to 75% mark-up.

Delivery

Getting your product to market

Some companies break down delivery costs so customers can see what they're paying for. Many do not and will simply quote a single cost to move products from one location to another.

You can sell your products through local groups that gather suppliers together to sell to consumers.

* Real Food Direct | *www.realfooddirect.co.uk*

* The Suffolk Providore | *www.thesuffolkprovidore.co.uk*

* Local Food Direct | *www.welovelocalfood.co.uk*

Fast-growing Worcestershire-based Muddy Boots uses a professional delivery company for nationwide delivery of its popular burgers and steaks, delivering local orders itself. Muddy Boots is quite open about how its delivery system works, even describing it on its website *www.muddybootsfoods.co.uk*. It's a model of honesty and goodwill towards the customer, and undoubtedly an effective approach.

First of all though: what will happen when you order?

1. You'll receive an automatic order confirmation email and then Roland, Sarah or Miranda will email you shortly afterwards to arrange the best delivery day for you. We will always deliver within 5 days unless requested otherwise.

2. We use APC Couriers for deliveries nationwide and we use the Muddy Boots van for local deliveries and those that we can bundle together to make a route.

3. We use polyboxes and ice packs for the orders with frozen items or cardboard boxes for the ambient products.

4. Unfortunately we're not able to specify a time when we use the courier company – to do this doubles the courier costs.

What we can do though, and what most people do with us, is pass on instructions to the courier driver for a safe place to leave the polybox at your address. Also whether it can be left with a neighbour. So long as the spot is in the shade, the polybox will keep the contents frozen until you get home. It really helps that people don't have to worry about being at home to receive it on a weekday.

So now to have a go at explaining delivery costs:

It's our goal to keep the delivery costs to as little as possible because then you'll hopefully use us again. We'll try and take on as much of the costs as we can ourselves without going so far so as not to make any money...! The days when "postage and packaging" was £2.95 are unfortunately far behind us because of fuel costs, credit card charges and general inflation on packaging, ice packs, cardboard etc.

Now this part is **not for you to worry about,** it's for us to factor into our own margins but we thought it might be interesting to list the costs (prices January 2012):

* APC Courier delivery is £6.40

* Polybox for anything frozen £1.30 or Cardboard box for ambient 57p

* Ice pack for anything frozen 18p

* Average bank charge per online transaction £1.03

* Average packaging inside the boxes 25p (bubble wrap for glass etc.)

* Staff time to process the order and pack it up approx. £2.15

So the total is £11.88; and we reckon we should take on most of that, so orders under £50 are £4.90 for delivery.

Then, we look at how we can afford to bring this down even more – orders over £50 mean that we're making a little more profit on the order (fitting more into a box whilst still only using one polybox for example, and one card charge and only a tiny bit more staff time, and so on) so we're going to try and offer free delivery over £50.

It is especially important to make sure that:

* food is transported in packaging or containers that protect it from contamination

* chilled and frozen foods are kept at the right temperature (some businesses use cool bags and boxes, or refrigerated vans)

* raw and ready-to-eat foods are kept apart

* vehicles used to transport food must be kept clean and in good repair.

* Muddy Boots | *www.muddybootsfoods.co.uk*
* APC Couriers | *www.apc-overnight.com*

FUNDING

You can raise money and finance for your business in many ways, from dipping into your own resources, borrowing from family, the bank or applying for a grant.

Friends and family

Friends and family may be the first people you approach for funding. Agreeing a written contract covering the amount borrowed and a payback schedule is vital so that everyone understands what is expected. It's very easy for relationships to get frayed by money issues, and businesses to disintegrate as a result.

Fund 101

If you're seeking up to £500 to boost your business, try applying to Enterprise Nation's Fund 101.

Businesses submit their case for receiving £50 to £500 to the readers of Enterprise Nation, who then vote on who gets the money. The number of votes required is equal to the amount of funding you're looking for. So to obtain £500 you need to secure 500 virtual votes.

If you get enough votes, the money is sent to you via PayPal. It's not a loan – the money is yours to keep, no strings attached. Your business is later profiled on Enterprise Nation, so readers can see how the money helped you.

★ *www.enterprisenation.com/fund101*

Banks and building societies

Book an appointment with a small business advisor at a couple of different high street banks. Take a smart, detailed copy of your business plan with you to talk it through. They will be keen to know what your business does and how you will make money from it.

Prepare yourself for the meeting by running through the presentation with a friend or colleague, and know your numbers.

TIP: It is a good idea to open a business bank account early on to avoid mixing up business and personal finances. You may need to provide a business plan and, if a limited company, a certificate of incorporation. (More on incorporating or registering your business in Chapter 6.) Find out more about requirements for opening a business bank account at the Business Link website: *bit.ly/hh3war*

Credit cards

It's riskier than other funding sources, but many businesses have started on the back of a credit card. There are plenty of competitive offers out there from credit card companies, all keen for your business. High interest rates on credit card debt make this a short-term route to funding, though.

Do make sure you don't miss repayments, and pay back the credit as soon as possible.

Grants

There are grants available from many different sources, including the government, charities such as The Prince's Trust, and the European Union.

* Business Link | *www.businesslink.gov.uk/grants*

* National Enterprise Network (with links to your local enterprise agency) | *www.nationalenterprisenetwork.org*

* j4b Grants | *www.j4bGrants.co.uk*
  Search the j4b database for business grants and community grants from a range of government and European funding sources.

* The Prince's Trust | *www.princes-trust.org*
  Provides practical and financial support to young people.

Graeme Kidd Memorial Bursary

The Graeme Kidd Memorial Bursary is a grant of up to £1,000 that aims to help young people develop their skills, experience and ultimately their career in food and drink. Applications are accepted from anyone within a 30-mile radius of Ludlow, Shropshire aged between 16 and 25. The fund is managed by Ludlow Food Festival.

A recent winner, Sam Bruce of Scrummy Bites, specialises in homemade food including cakes, quiches and tea breads. He is in no doubt about the impact the bursary had on his business. He says:

> "Winning gave me much more confidence to pursue my ideas and take my business to the next level. The financial boost helped me with advertising and equipment."

Since winning, Sam has launched a new Garden Tea Room in his local town and started supplying his products to shops in the area. Regularly asked to do parties and events he has also featured on *Market Kitchen* on the Good Food TV channel.

The award was created in memory of Graeme Kidd, a leading member of the Ludlow community, and one of the founders of the famous Ludlow Food Festival.

* Ludlow Food Festival | *www.foodfestival.co.uk*
* Graeme Kidd Memorial Bursary | *www.foodfestival.co.uk*
* Scrummy Bites | *www.scrummybites.co.uk*

Landskills

Lantra (*www.lantra.co.uk*) provides rural businesses with improved access to skills and training courses.

For example, Landskills East (*www.landskillseast.co.uk*) covers and provides courses in food photography, using social media and new product development. Landskills West Midlands provides courses on adding value to meat by creating interesting and innovative pies, patés and terrines, and sausage-making, bacon-curing, pastrami and ham.

The Prince's Trust

Developed by HRH The Prince of Wales, The Prince's Trust (*www.princes-trust.org.uk*) gives practical and financial support to young people with troubled backgrounds, developing key workplace skills such as confidence and motivation. They work with 13 to 30-year-olds who have struggled at school, been in care, are long-term unemployed or have been in trouble with the law.

The Prince's Countryside Fund

Also backed by HRH The Prince of Wales, The Prince's Countryside Fund has three goals:

* to improve the sustainability of British farming and rural communities, targeting the areas of greatest need

* to reconnect consumers with countryside issues

* to support farming and rural crisis charities through a dedicated emergency funding stream.

The business of food comes into this quite a lot. For example, the fund is now working with Hampshire Fare, the county food group of Hampshire. With local pig farmers currently under threat, together they hope to preserve the 'Hampshire hog' by helping farmers and pig owners add value to their pork through cured meats.

By uniting producers and covering the initial charcuterie training and marketing costs, the aim is to develop a new marque and sell the products at local events and through shops and restaurants, ensuring a sustainable future for Hampshire pig farmers. Keep an eye out for similar schemes near you.

* Hampshire Fare | *www.hampshirefare.co.uk*
* The Prince's Countryside Fund | *www.princescountrysidefund.org.uk*

Investors

Venture capitalists and angel investors generally offer *established* businesses the money they need for further development and expansion, so they're perhaps more relevant further on in your business's life.

Nevertheless, it doesn't do any harm to take a look at them at this stage. Investors will be looking to take a slice of equity in your business, unlike banks, but will be able to invest expertise as well as money.

* Angels Den | *www.angelsden.com*
* Funding Circle | *www.fundingcircle.com*
* The UK Business Angels Association | *www.ukbusinessangelsassociation.org.uk*

Local organisations and community groups

Local organisations and community groups exist across the country with a focus on local projects. For example:

Foundation East is a community finance organisation providing business loans of up to £50,000 to existing and start-up businesses in Cambridge, Bedfordshire, Suffolk, Hertfordshire, Norfolk and Essex.

★ *www.foundationeast.org*

StartUp Shropshire is a campaign to help aspiring start-up enterprises, sole traders and freelance contractors. This local movement was inspired by StartUp Britain and is developing a forum of local businesses, councils, entrepreneurs and individuals. These will all combine their energies to help new start-ups in the county.

★ *www.startupshropshire.org*

Crowdfunding

Crowdfunding uses the power of social media such as Facebook and Twitter to generate interest about a particular business idea. Funders then contribute small amounts of money to a particular company they feel has a chance of success in return for a 'reward' usually related to the project. Check out *www.zopa.com*, *www.crowdfunder.co.uk* and *www.kickstarter.com*.

CASE STUDY
HANDMADE FUDGE COMPANY

Michelle Mapplethorpe and her husband already had two businesses in the Isles of Scilly, a fish-and-chip shop and a takeaway selling pasties, cakes and fudge. People kept asking if their fudge was handmade. At the time it wasn't, but Michelle realised that she would sell more fudge if it was – and that's how their third business, the Handmade Fudge Shop, was born.

Fudge-making on a commercial scale is technically complicated and recipes are closely guarded secrets. Michelle started making fudge in the home kitchen commercially after her children had grown up and left home, "as it would have been difficult to manage fudge-making trays with cooking for the family".

Michelle credits Taste of the West and the Isles of Scilly Local Action Group for helping get the business off the ground – with insurance, business advice, and assistance on bidding to sell their fudge into the London 2012 Olympic Games.

* Handmade Fudge Shop | *www.thehandmadefudgeshop.co.uk*

* Taste of the West | *www.tasteofthewest.co.uk*

* Isles of Scilly Local Action Group | *www.ios.fundingsouthwest.co.uk*

CHAPTER 6

Registering Your Business

W ith a business plan under your belt, the next stage is registering your food business with a number of authorities.

WHAT'S THE BEST FORM OF COMPANY FOR ME?

There are a number of types of company. After you've chosen the one that is best for you, you'll need to contact and inform HM Revenue & Customs (HMRC) at *www.hmrc.gov.uk*. You may also need to register with Companies House.

Here are the options:

Self-employed sole trader

Being a sole trader is the simplest way to run a business: it does not involve paying any registration fees, maintaining records and accounts is straightforward, and you get to keep all the profits. However, you are personally liable for any debts that your business runs up – a risky option for businesses that require a lot of investment.

Partnership

In a partnership, two or more people share the risks, costs and responsibilities of being in business. Each partner is self-employed and takes a share of the profits. Usually, each partner shares in the decision-making and is personally responsible for any debts that the business runs up.

Unlike a limited company, a partnership has no legal existence distinct from the partners themselves.

Limited Liability Partnership (LLP)

An LLP is similar to an ordinary partnership – in that a number of individuals or limited companies share in the risks, costs, responsibilities and profits of the business.

The difference is that liability is limited to the amount of money they have invested in the business and to any personal guarantees they have given to raise finance. This means that members have some protection if the business runs into trouble.

Limited Liability Companies

Limited companies exist in their own right. This means the company's finances are separate from the personal finances of their owners.

Shareholders may be individuals or other companies. They are not responsible for the company's debts unless they have given guarantees (of a bank loan, for example). However, they may lose the money they have invested in the company if it fails.

Franchise

Buying a franchise is a way of taking advantage of the success of an established business. As the 'franchisee', you buy a licence to use the name, products, services and management support systems of the 'franchisor' company. This licence normally covers a particular geographical area and runs for a limited time, after which it should be renewable as long as you meet the terms of the franchise agreement.

SOURCE: BUSINESS LINK (*www.businesslink.gov.uk*)

Many high street food and catering businesses – e.g. McDonald's – are built on the franchise model, with local operators paying a regular fee to 'head office' for a variety of services.

Franchisees generally pay a joining fee; an upfront amount of money which covers fixed costs such as fitting out a commercial kitchen. You'll also need cash for working capital, covering variable costs such as staff wages, utilities and supplies. If you are considering buying a catering franchise, check that the company is a member of the industry standards body, the British Franchise Association. The BFA is full of useful advice if you go down this route.

Bear in mind that few catering franchises are home-based, needing larger catering premises to serve customers. Some more modest-scale ones include:

* Jamie at Home | *www.jamieathome.com*
* My Secret Kitchen | *www.mysecretkitchen.co.uk*

* The Pampered Chef | *www.pamperedchef.co.uk*
* British Franchise Association | *www.thebfa.org*

ENVIRONMENTAL HEALTH REGISTRATION

You must also register your premises with the environmental health service at your local authority at least 28 days before opening.

Who needs to register?

Registration applies to most types of food business, including catering businesses run from home and mobile or temporary premises, such as stalls and vans. If you use more than one premise, you will need to register all of them.

How much will it cost?

Registration is free.

How can you register?

Registration is simple. You can either download an application from your local authority's website and then email, fax or post it to the food team in the environmental health department. Or, if your local authority offers it, you can fill out the form entirely online.

Contact your local authority to find out more.

The government's Food Standards Agency offers plenty of registration advice at *www.food.gov.uk*.

CASE STUDY
SOUTH DEVON CHILLI FARM

Business partners Steve Waters and Jason Nickels met through a mutual love of chillies. Jason was importing dried chillies, repackaging and selling them via a website, while Steve was growing chillies for his own use in a garden greenhouse.

Their business, South Devon Chilli Farm, started as a hobby. The two friends rented a polytunnel and started growing chilli plants while holding down full-time jobs. The fledgling plants were checked in the evening after work and at weekends.

When harvest time bought a glut of chillies – far too many for family and friends – they took a stall at a local farmers' market and cooked up a few sauces to bottle and sell. "They were very popular," says Steve. And the business was underway. With one snag: they hadn't registered with the local environmental health officer.

"In hindsight," says Steve, "we should have contacted them as soon as we started making the sauces. We only involved them after we had been to a few markets, when a fellow stallholder mentioned it to us."

Fortunately, far from being a nightmarish process that they feared might jeopardise their young business, it was a simple and encouraging step.

"We were worried about not having enough sinks, or about the dog," says Steve. "But it was fine. The inspectors were happy with everything we were doing to prevent contamination. We felt they were there to help build our business and support us. They really are there to encourage, not put you off."

★   South Devon Chilli Farm | *www.southdevonchillifarm.co.uk*

What else do you need to do?

* If you expect to produce a lot of waste, get in touch with your local authority to organise waste and recycling collections and get appropriate training and tools (if relevant). It could cost you more money if you don't.

* You might need to register as self-employed and/or register for Valued Added Tax (VAT). (See Chapter 7.)

* If you want to make changes to your premises, you might need planning permission (see page 109 onwards for more information).

* You'll need to pay business rates on most premises and acquire licences for certain activities, such as selling or supplying alcohol or selling hot food between 11pm and 5am – not usually relevant for a home-based business.

Starting-up checklist

★ Have you registered your premises?

★ Do the design and construction of your premises meet legal requirement?

★ Are you aware of the main General Food Law Regulations? The government's Food Standards Agency (*www.food.gov.uk/enforcement*) has plenty of current information about relevant legislation affecting the production and sale of food.

★ Do you keep written records of all the suppliers that provide you with food or ingredients?

★ Have you put food safety management procedures in place and are you keeping up-to-date records of these?

★ Do you and your staff understand the principles of good food hygiene?

★ Have you considered health and safety and fire safety arrangements?

★ Have you registered as self-employed?

★ Do you need to register for VAT?

★ Are you keeping records of all your business income and expenses?

★ Do you describe food and drink accurately?

★ Do you need to apply for a licence to sell alcohol, for entertainment, for selling hot food and drink late at night, or selling food on the street?

SOURCE: FOOD STANDARDS AGENCY (*www.food.gov.uk*)

WHAT TO CALL YOUR COMPANY AND HOW TO PROTECT ITS NAME

Choosing a name for your business is an important and enjoyable creative task. Your name informs customers, projects your and your company's personality and enhances your business profile and image – it's an important role for just a couple of words. It must grab people's attention.

It can be so much fun that you might spend hours and hours looking for that special name. Just don't get obsessive about it.

Make a list of possible names and words: jumble them up, ask friends and family and decide whether each one reflects your brand. Do you want a local, homely, national, traditional or modern flavour to the name?

THE RED ONE: In 2006, children's food company Ella's Kitchen (*www.ellaskitchen.co.uk*) launched its first products, two organic Smoothie Fruits called The Red One and The Yellow One – names inspired by the founder's own children. While testing the products at home, the young son of founder Paul Lindley asked for "the red one – because it's like a fire engine and looks fun." The name stuck.

Alongside your company name, you'll need a logo. The logo might just be the company's name, or you could go for something more iconic. The logo will be used on everything from business cards to menus, websites and general marketing literature. Make sure it's one you're happy with.

Using a local graphic designer will keep costs down, but you should be clear about your company and what it stands for before commissioning any design.

"While it may be tempting to try to stamp your individual personality on your business name, there are many other issues to consider. Being objective and choosing a name that reflects your business strategy can be more valuable, especially as your business develops."

– Business Link

EXAMPLE: A popular farmers' market in Birmingham's heritage Jewellery Quarter is called 24 Carrots (*www.24carrots.org.uk*), a pun on the area's long association with precious metals.

It may be worth avoiding naming your company after yourself or a single product as it can complicate future growth. So if you're a baker, perhaps refrain from using words like biscuit, cake or cupcake in your title as this will pigeonhole your company. And steer clear of trendy names – what's in fashion today might not be tomorrow.

Always consider how your name will sound spoken over the telephone or at events. Can potential customers pronounce and spell it easily?

Names and the web

When choosing a name, remember that you'll also need to choose an online domain name (or URL) to go with it:

1. Is the domain name available?

2. Does it (and your name) contain relevant keywords?

3. Does it (and your name) contain a term that people would search for?

Legal aspects

Names used by sole traders and unincorporated businesses are known as business names, while the names of incorporated limited businesses are referred to as company names.

Although you won't need to register it, your business name must comply with the Business Names Act of 1985. Company names must be registered at Companies House and comply with the Companies Act of 1985.

Is someone else using the name?

Check that someone else isn't already using your chosen name through the following free resources:

* The Companies House register, which lists the names of limited companies and limited liability partnerships (LLPs).

* The Trade Marks Journal published by the UK Intellectual Property Office (UK-IPO).

* Membership directories for chambers of commerce or professional bodies.

* Trade and telephone directories.

CASE STUDY
Mrs Tinks

When Julia Boddy became a full-time mum in 2009, after being made redundant, she had spent almost ten years building a career in HR and training. Suddenly finding herself at home with three young children was, in many ways, just what she wanted and needed. But not in every way.

> "It was very hard. I wanted to make the most of being at home with the children but I also knew I wanted to go back to work and promised myself I would try and do something different. I only decided what that 'something' was after spending endless hours in the kitchen, cooking for the family."

Julia was a big fan of seeing her children enjoy her food, but like most people wanted a break now and then with kids' ready meals. The only problem: "a limited range and no success – the children didn't like them".

> "I thought I could do a much better job. I was never going to win *Masterchef* but I knew my food tasted great and was healthy and fresh. So I came up with Mrs Tinks – fresh and tasty meals that children love to eat and that parents want them to eat."

Julia initially thought that she could start "by making the meals at home and then selling them through some local delis and shops". With hindsight this was a little "naive", she says; "the amount of things you have to have in place to be able to make and sell meals to be eaten by children is vast."

"There are documents to create, processes to follow, courses to attend, food tests to arrange ... The list was endless and it soon became clear that producing the food at home was not an option."

Thankfully she discovered consultancy The Olive Grows, where she cooks the food and "gets invaluable guidance and support".

"There have been times when I have felt I could never get this to work and having people I can turn to has saved me on many, many occasions. Coming from a non-foodie background I have found that listening to people who know more than me and have much more experience has been the best way to learn!"

* Mrs Tinks | *www.tinksfood.com*
* The Olive Grows | *www.theolivegrows.org*

Protecting your name and products

You can protect your name in a variety of ways.

* **Patents:** These are, essentially, what makes things work. For example, says the Intellectual Property Office (IPO), "the chemical formula of your favourite fizzy drink."

* **Trademarks:** These are "signs (like words and logos) that distinguish goods and services in the marketplace."

* **Designs:** What a logo or product looks like.

* **Copyright:** An automatic right that comes into existence for anything written or recorded.

Before commissioning an IP expert to help you with this, learn the basics from the IPO website, use the British Library Business and IP Centre in London, and consult fellow entrepreneurs for advice. This all needs to be done early in your business's life.

One way to protect your company name is to register as a limited company – even if you're trading as a sole trader or partnership. The company name can simply remain dormant until you wish to change your trading status.

Once your business name is in use, make occasional checks to ensure that no one else is setting up nearby or in the same line of business using a similar name.

* She's Ingenious | *www.shesingenious.org*

* Business Link | *www.businesslink.gov.uk*

* Companies House | *www.companieshouse.gov.uk*

* UK Intellectual Property Office | *www.ipo.gov.uk*

* British Library Business & IP Centre | *www.bl.uk/bipc*

* Local Food Direct | *www.welovelocalfood.co.uk*

CHAPTER 7

Accountants, Tax and Insurance

N o matter how small your food business, there will be paperwork. Most of it will be generated by the financial side of things, and it's best to keep on top of it from the start.

ACCOUNTANTS AND TAX

You'll need to be organised and keep a **clear record of your business expenses** separate from your living expenses. This means, for example, that the utility costs of operating your commercial kitchen should be kept separate from your home utility bills. When tax day arrives, you can actually write off these costs as a deduction. You can also write off some of your travel expenses.

You can either file your own tax accounts online or through your accounts. **Make sure you speak with an accountant** to take advantage of tax benefits and ensure you are not abusing the write-offs.

Emily Coltman of *FreeAgent.com*, author of *Finance for Small Business*, says that "accountants for entrepreneurs are rather like bicarbonate of soda for bakers – not glamorous, but a vital ingredient for success."

★ A good accountant **will give you peace of mind** that your business's tax affairs are in proper order. This is not to be underestimated, particularly when you think what a wilderness the UK's tax system is.

* Having your accounts and tax return prepared professionally provides **additional security** if you want to borrow money, or go into a joint venture with another business. Some lenders may want to see accounts prepared by a qualified accountant before they'll consider lending you any cash.

* A good accountant will also **act as your agent** with HMRC and **field any awkward queries**. They'll also be at your side if HMRC visit for an inspection.

* A good accountant will understand why you're in business, and **advise and charge you appropriately**. If your business is a hobby business and your accountant tries to push you into forming a limited company, alarm bells should start ringing.

* Free Agent | *www.freeagent.com*
* HMRC | *www.hmrc.gov.uk*
* *Finance for Small Business* | *www.brightwordpublishing.com/finance*

VAT registration

One issue to consider when starting out is VAT (Value Added Tax) registration. VAT is a tax that you pay when you buy goods and services in the EU, including the UK. If you have to pay VAT on something, it will normally be included in the price you see.

If you are under the current limit you do not need to charge VAT. The trigger is based on your turnover – you should register if you expect your turnover to exceed £77,000 (2012/13 tax year). You can register for VAT at any time.

Whether or not you need to include VAT in your prices, and at what rate, depends on a number of different things:

* For businesses that are VAT registered, there are some key rules. If you sell food or drink to be consumed on your premises, or if you supply hot takeaway food, you must charge VAT at the standard rate on these products.

* Normally, you do not need to charge VAT on cold takeaway food and drink, but there are some products where standard-rate VAT always applies, such as crisps, sweets and bottled water.

* If you process someone else's food products to produce new goods that are zero-rated for VAT, then your services are zero-rated for VAT too.

* Caterers that supply food to a school or hospital may not have to charge VAT.

Check your VAT situation and contact HMRC at *www.hmrc.gov.uk/VAT*.

CASE STUDY
CHOKOLIT

Start-up chocolatier Louis Barnett started his business in his parent's kitchen at the age of 11. By the time he left his teenage years behind him he was running a business supplying chocolate around the world. Louis became the youngest ever supplier to Waitrose at 13 years of age, Sainsbury's at 14 and Selfridges at 15.

Says Louis:

"Our success is based on the quality and taste of our products. Made using no palm oil, no artificial flavours, colours or additives – it's not what we put in our chocolate, it's what we leave out that makes it so special."

A popular public speaker and mentor, here are some of his key business principles:

★ You don't make mistakes, **you only learn lessons**.

★ **Everything happens for a reason.** Lessons learned from the early stage of a business can be used to enhance business dealings later on.

★ **Consider what the company stands for** and what are its values. Take every aspect of your business and pull it apart to improve it.

★ **Don't waste months** and months worrying about what might or might not happen.

* Lessons learnt from one day might not become apparent for days, weeks, months or even years. **Be alive to learning!**

* **Contracts: if it's not on paper, it doesn't exist.** Get everything written down – Louis has a ten-page contract for when he's hired as a speaker. Get it down on paper – trading terms, non-disclosure, booking forms, product order forms, etc.

* **Go global.** Consider exporting your produce. There is strong interest in British products around the world. The UK government agency UKTI (*www.ukti.gov.uk*) can help here. Louis sees a strong, long-term future in exporting to Singapore, Indonesia, Malaysia and Latin America.

* **Think big.** Louis spent three hours trying to convince a farm shop in England to take (on sale and return) just 60 bars of his chocolate. He also had to provide marketing support to interest the retailer (all at his own cost). Louis then visited a shop in New York and spent 15 minutes with a buyer, who immediately ordered six pallets! Direct your efforts thoughtfully to maximise sales.

* **Support charities.** Louis is an active supporter of several charities, including protecting the jungle environment of orangutans in Sumatra, which is being taken over by palm oil estates.

* Chokolit | *www.chokolit.co.uk*

INSURANCE

Accidents do happen, no matter how careful you are. Insurance is not a cost you can avoid. Plan for it from the start.

* As the business owner, **you are held responsible for any harm** that comes to your employees, visitors to your home, or consumers of your products.

* Look at the levels for *public liability* that different insurance companies offer. Usually the lowest level is £1 million, but **most insurance brokers will recommend that those in the catering trade take at least £5 million in public liability cover**. Check with your local council's environmental health officer for the current total value of coverage required.

* All farmers' markets will **require you to have product liability and public liability insurance**.

* Underinsuring a business can seriously affect the amount of money paid out in the event of a claim. It is important to **have the correct level of cover for all assets** – including premises, stock and equipment, mobile shops and hot food vans.

TIP: Read through your business insurance policy carefully to understand what is covered and what is not. Keep your insurer or broker informed about any significant changes to your business which may affect your policy so they can advise of necessary amendments.

Product liability insurance

Product liability insurance protects your business if anyone is hurt or killed or their property is damaged by goods you have made, sold or repaired. You could be held liable for damage or injury caused by defects in your products' design or manufacture even if you haven't been negligent.

The food industry is considered high risk and you should arrange cover for your business. Product liability cover is often included with public liability insurance. Liability is not just limited to *your* products; your company could be sued for serving contaminated food sourced from a supplier.

If you serve a birthday cake baked, for example, by a friend of your client who does not have product insurance, the client needs to sign a liability waiver. This should be written with help from your insurance broker. It means that your client and guests waive any rights to legal action against you should the cake be contaminated.

Public liability insurance

Public liability insurance covers damages and legal costs resulting from injury, death or damage to property caused to members of the public by any of your business activities.

You're more likely to need this if customers or the public visit your premises, e.g. if you run a shop. Bespoke insurance policies are available for the catering industry. For example, if you have a catering trailer it will need to be insured for accidental damage, fire and theft. Optional cover might include material damage to stock.

Insurance in the home

If you're operating your business from home, you might need to add special measures to your policy:

* You'll need **employer's liability insurance** if you employ anyone at your home, even part-time.

* You may need a **specialised home worker's policy** that will cover you for business interruption. This would pay out for providing a temporary office if, for example, your home was flooded.

* Consider taking out **permanent health/accident insurance** that will pay out a regular income if you are unable to work because of an accident or serious illness.

Some companies offer a home-worker package, which includes cover for most items you'd expect in a more traditional commercial policy such as business contents and stock, goods in transit, and legal expenses. Such packages should also offer you the chance to upgrade insurance with affordable extras, including home insurance, commercial liabilities and personal accident cover.

Check the Nationwide Caterers Association (*www.ncassinsurance.co.uk*) for more details.

Business continuity/interruption

You can help by creating your own **business continuity plan** (BCP), providing simple, inexpensive action points should your company be faced with crisis (from illness to flooding, fire, IT breakdown or severe weather). With a plan in hand, you should be able to keep your customers supplied.

Check out Business Link for advice on developing a crisis management plan: *businesslink.gov.uk/crisismanagement*.

ADMIN Q&A

Lastly, here's a quick rundown of the rules and regulations of being a home-based business.

Q. Do I need planning permission?

A. You'll need planning permission to base your business at home if you answer 'yes' to any of these questions:

★ will your home no longer be used mainly as a private residence?

★ will your business result in a marked rise in traffic or people calling?

★ will your business involve any activities that are unusual in a residential area?

* will your business disturb the neighbours at unreasonable hours or create other forms of nuisance such as noise or smells?

If your house is pretty much going to remain a house, with your business quietly accommodated within it, then permission shouldn't be required. If you're unsure, contact your local council to seek their views.

* Planning Portal | *www.planningportal.gov.uk*

Q. Do I need to tell the local authority I'm working from home?

A. This depends on whether you pass the planning test. If you need planning permission you'll have to inform your local authority.

Working from home could mean the part of the property used for work may be liable to business rates (also known as non-domestic rates) whilst the remainder of the property will continue to be liable to council tax (although an alteration may be made to its banding). Assessments are organised by the Valuation Office.

To decide whether or not part of your property is liable for business rates there are a number of things to consider, including the extent and frequency of the non-domestic (business), use of the room (or rooms), and any modifications made to the property to accommodate that use.

If your property needs to be assessed for business rates, your local Valuation Office will work out a rateable value for the part that is used for business purposes.

* Business Link | *www.businesslink.gov.uk/businessrates*

Q. Do I need to tell the landlord?

A. Yes, it's best to let them know you'll be working from home. Some tenancy agreements prohibit it, though it should be negotiable.

Q. Do I need to inform my mortgage provider?

A. Yes, it's best to let them know – even though it shouldn't mean any change in the mortgage repayment.

Q. What about my insurance provider? Do they need to know?

A. Yes, do inform your insurance company. Tell them about the equipment and stock you have at home. An upgrade from domestic to a business policy is not usually expensive so don't be put off in making this call. Your insurance provider is likely to recommend that you also take out public liability insurance in case anyone who comes to visit suffers an injury in or around your home premises.

Q. Do I need protection for when customers and contacts come to visit?

A. Yes, carry out a health and safety check, which is easy to do by following the steps set out by the Health and Safety Executive in their *Homeworking* guide (pdf available at *bit.ly/aGDc8N*).

★ Health and Safety Executive | *www.hse.gov.uk*

Q. Should I tell the neighbours?

A. It's always best to keep neighbours on your side. They can easily get annoyed if large trucks and vans start delivering early in the morning or street parking is made difficult. Perhaps your business will generate lots of smells and noise – if it does, warn the neighbours and perhaps keep them sweet with some of your produce.

PART TWO

Running Your Food Business

CHAPTER 8

Being a Home-based Business

Right – paperwork and bureaucracy out of the way, it's time to start cooking!

Working with limited space and equipment, meeting health and hygiene codes and regulations, competing with caterers who have access to commercial kitchens or shops is all part of being a home-based business. This chapter will take you through how to accomplish it successfully.

KITCHEN LAYOUT TIPS

The kitchen will be the heart of your business, so it's a good idea to create the best working environment you can.

Be mindful of keeping all working areas clean and maintaining top level hygiene standards, particularly when preparing different foodstuffs to avoid cross-contamination.

TIP: When planning from scratch, kitchen designers often start with the concept of a work triangle, in which the sink, cooker and fridge form the corners. Hopefully these three key units will at least be fairly close to each other.

It's likely that your kitchen is already installed, and it's probably not necessary to spend money on a new one at the start of your business. If there is room, perhaps install a work island. Fitting an extra sink on the island will help separate food preparation areas from the main sink, oven and cooker.

If you're right-handed, you'll want the prep space to the right of the sink; if you're left-handed, you'll want to place your prep space to the left.

Here are some ways of ensuring you make the best possible use of your space:

★ **Sturdy, foldaway tables** are good short-term solutions to limited counter space. Wall-papering tables are too wobbly, though, and not suitable.

★ Ideally your **storage for plates and glasses** should be near your dishwasher so you don't have far to go to put things away. Consider installing a commercial dishwasher if time is of the essence. These run faster and have more space for items.

★ **Install the largest refrigerator** you can, perhaps in the garage, and perhaps alongside an extra deepfreeze.

★ **Rubbish and waste should be removed regularly**, at least daily, from the kitchen and prep area and stored in a designated area, protected against infestations of insects or even rodents.

★ In the short term, you can **hire equipment** for specific or one-off contracts. In the medium term, you might consider leasing equipment.

★ **Wire-rack shelving** can be purchased by DIY stores. Easy to install and keep clean, the shelving must be sturdy.

★ **Regularly used kitchen utensils** should be easily accessible. They can be hung from the ceiling for easier visibility and access.

★ **Garden centres often sell trolleys** which can be stacked with utensils or ingredients and wheeled into food preparation areas when needed. Useful for smaller kitchens.

★ **A good quality, accurate weighing scale is a must** to ensure product consistency. Like most regularly used tools, this should be kept handy and preferably in one place to avoid constant movement and possible breakage.

★ If you have toddlers at home while you are preparing your products, **create a dismountable play area** close to your workspace so you can keep your eye on them while you work.

★ Whether you have a gas or electric cooker, **ensure that the thermostat works** or keep an oven thermometer handy.

★ Mixers will get lots of use, so **invest in a larger, stand mixer** with a sufficiently large blow and high powered (wattage) motor for a longer life.

★ **Store cookbooks and paperwork out of the kitchen.** They absorb grease and moisture, quickly making them unusable.

★ If you have a central light but want to **shine light on a different area,** put it on a longer cord then put a small hook into the ceiling above where you need the light, and just clip it over.

★ Similarly, buy an **inexpensive clip light** and clamp it on where you need extra task light.

CASE STUDY
MUKAASE FOODS

Growing up in Ghana and helping mum out in the kitchen gave Christiana Asiama the love of food and technical knowledge that lies behind her business, Mukaase Foods, in Telford, Shropshire.

Mukaase, an African word for kitchen, is based in Christiana's dining room, which has been converted into a commercial kitchen. Start-up support came from Harper Adams University in Shropshire and from the regional food organisation, Heart of England Fine Foods (HEFF).

When a large order needs fulfilling, Christiana uses the facilities at Harper Adams.

Mukaase started by offering meals-on-wheels to local businesses. Since then it has grown by supplying local farm shops, including a showcase retail outlet for the West Midlands managed by HEFF in Shrewsbury.

Christiana's husband runs the administrative side of the business, while Christiana cooks up traditional Ghanaian dishes, including jerk chicken with jollop rice.

* Mukaase Foods | *www.mukaasefoods.co.uk*

* Harper Adams | *www.harper-adams.ac.uk*

* HEFF | *www.heff.co.uk*

Colours

Today, kitchens are often the focal point of our homes: where we eat, work and entertain. To create the right mood for your home-business kitchen, consider carefully which colours you might use to inspire a range of different moods.

Here are some quick tips from the colour experts at Farrow & Ball:

* In general, **cool colours** make a room feel larger and give a more formal look to a room.

* **Warm colours** make a room feel smaller and give a more relaxed feel.

* For a **restful look**, it is best to use a single neutral colour. Contrasts and strong colours create a distraction and take away from a feeling of calm.

* If you are looking to **expand on light and space,** use the lightest colour on the biggest area. Contrast this with darker woodwork to make the walls look even lighter.

Farrow & Ball have recreated the Cook's Blue colour, often found in kitchens and larders during the 19th century in the belief that flies never land on it.

* Farrow & Ball | *www.farrow-ball.com*

SAVING MONEY IN THE KITCHEN

Your fridge, freezer and oven will all be working overtime in your home-business kitchen. Here are a few tips for keeping electricity and gas costs down:

★ Use a vacuum cleaner to **clean the condenser coils** at the back or underneath your fridge or freezer. Thick dust can reduce their efficiency by up to 25%, according to consumer organisation Which? (*www.which.co.uk*).

★ **Check for eco-cycles** on your domestic appliances. Designed to use less water and electricity than traditional daily programs, eco-cycles are found on most modern large kitchen appliances.

★ **Keep your freezer well stocked** to reduce electricity demands.

Go green

Renovate and recycle to reduce waste and save money. There are hundreds of small ways you can run an environmentally friendly business.

Perhaps your local food group offers a green accreditation scheme. West Midlands food group Heart of England Fine Foods (HEFF) has teamed up with a local consultancy to help food and drink producers gain environmental accreditations. Check your local food group to see whether they offer environmental training or accreditation.

National food groups

* England | *www.englishfoodanddrinkalliance.co.uk*

* Northern Ireland | *www.nifda.co.uk*

* Scotland | *www.scotlandfoodanddrink.org*

* Wales | *www.walesthetruetaste.co.uk*

HEALTH AND SAFETY

While 'health and safety' is often an unwanted intrusion in everyday life, you cannot afford to take it lightly if you're producing food and drink at home. A lot may seem like common sense, but there is no harm in giving common sense a helping hand. The UK government's Food Safety Agency offers advice on issues such as kitchen hygiene and legislative changes to health and safety laws.

Handling – six tips to keep your food safe

1. Date and label your stock and rotate it, particularly in the freezer

2. Wash your hands, and look after your personal health

3. Keep working surfaces, utensils and tools clean

4. Buy ingredients from credible and reliable suppliers

5. If in doubt, throw the food away

6. Keep yourself and staff up-to-date with hygiene legislation through your local environmental health officer.

Food preparation areas

Here is a checklist from the Food Safety Agency for rooms where you use ingredients and cook:

Floors and walls

Floors and walls must be maintained in a 'sound condition', easy to clean and disinfect. In practice, this means that floors and walls should be smooth, hard-wearing, washable and in a good state of repair.

Ceilings

Ceilings must be constructed and finished in a way that prevents dirt from building up and reduces condensation, mould and shedding of particles.

Windows

Windows and any other openings (such as doors) that can be opened to the outside must be fitted, where necessary, with insect-proof screens that can be removed easily for cleaning.

Doors

Doors must be easy to clean and, where necessary, disinfect.

Surfaces

Surfaces (including surfaces of equipment) in areas where food is handled, particularly those that are touched by food, must be maintained in a sound condition and be easy to clean and, where necessary, to disinfect.

Facilities for cleaning equipment

You must have adequate facilities to allow cleaning, disinfecting and storing of utensils and equipment. Hot and cold water should be at hand.

Facilities for washing food

Every sink (or similar facility) for washing food must have an adequate supply of hot and/or cold drinking-quality water.

Storage materials

Storage containers should be of catering standard, and foil should be aluminium and food grade (it will tell you on the packaging if it is the correct grade for food).

Acidic foods such as fruit should be covered with clingfilm and not foil. If you use a microwave, never cover food with foil but use catering-strength clingfilm. If the film melts into the food, or gets splattered with hot fat, the food will get contaminated. ''

* Food Safety Agency | *www.food.gov.uk*

Best Cook in Country Living's Kitchen Table Talent awards

Helen Damer of Lanarkshire, Scotland won 'Best Cook' in the Kitchen Table Talent Awards 2011 run by *Country Living* Magazine. Her story was published in the September 2011 issue of *Country Living* Magazine and on the blog *www.kitchentabletalent.com*. Here it is ...

"

Everyone was in agreement, Helen's sausages (particularly the pork and fennel) were succulent, finely flavoured and absolutely delicious. Surely the work of an expert butcher, a long-time producer? No, Helen only began rearing pigs in January 2011, renting woodland from a neighbour, mincing the meat on a borrowed machine and experimenting with different recipes in her kitchen.

Her story is a long one: a career in catering with John Lewis, taking her from the Pennines to Scotland then, when she started a family, she took a break from work and began baking and preserving: "One year there were so many raspberries along the banks of the Clyde I was making raspberry vodka for gifts. Friends open my jam cupboard door and tell me I should set up a farm shop with all my homemade produce. When I made the *Country Living* marmalade recipe my local shop offered to sell it." She longed to keep hens and now has a brood (plus ducks and quails). Keeping pigs was the natural next step. "I chose Berkshires – a traditional rare breed known for delicious pork and crackling. It is also a good-natured pig that the children are happy to handle."

Helen began to develop the flavours of her sausages, using herbs or honey and mustard or her favourite – pork with minced apples and her own apple jelly. "I went on a pig-keeping course and now I want to turn my hobby into a successful business, selling half-pigs as well as sausage and bacon products." She's already had a go at pancetta and pork pies. "I am determined to get the pastry just right," she says. "I also want to try a recipe for a rhubarb and pork open pie that sounds delicious." A local butcher has cured her latest pig for bacon and hams and she already has orders from family and friends. Recognising that there are a lot of people selling pork she plans to make hers stand out by including recipes for the less well-known cuts, alongside fresh herbs and a jar of her homemade jelly.

SOURCE: COUNTRY LIVING KITCHEN TABLE TALENT AWARDS

CREATING YOUR PERFECT WORK ENVIRONMENT

There'll be plenty of distractions while you're working from home, so to minimise their impact try and dedicate an area in the house that functions as your home office.

This space could be in your attic, under the stairs or in your (insulated and carpeted!) shed or garden office. To make the most of your garden office, check out the Shedworking blog (*www.shedworking.co.uk*). Business support website Smarta (*www.smarta.com*) also offers a few tips on how to organise your home office.

Kitchen incubators

Kitchen incubators are shared commercial kitchens that are available to rent on a short or long-term basis.

Some start-up food businesses use them to learn about the business, being mentored by and sharing ideas with the management and fellow entrepreneurs, or if planning rules prevent them using their home-kitchen. They're also great for when you want to start expanding, or if an unusual job requires more space.

Contact your local food group to find your local incubator kitchen. Some are privately run for profit, while others are associated with colleges and universities. These kitchens will charge fees, on a scale depending on what services you need. As a complete start-up you may be able to take up business or production support.

* Harper Adams University College | *www.harper-adams.ac.uk*

* Ludlow Food Centre | *www.ludlowfoodcentre.co.uk*

* The Olive Grows | *www.theolivegrows.org*

Food Funnel

Creative agency Jump To! has developed a new service to help artisan and food-based businesses rapidly access markets and scale up in size. Known as the Food Funnel, it helps connect young businesses with large retail outlets, media contacts and food trend-setters and spotters. Run by Mark Glynne-Jones, Jump To! has worked with brands and producers including Bacheldre Mill in Powys, Wales and Tyrrells English Crisps.

* Jump To! | *www.jumpto.co.uk*

Village halls and community centres

Many village halls and community centres have kitchens available for hire. It's good to have people using and supporting community facilities.

These spaces would only be suitable for short-term projects, but come with the advantage that they will most probably have the necessary health certificates. It's advisable to have a formal, written agreement between you and the facility owners.

Commercial spaces

Many catering companies or food producers start off working in commercial kitchens around the establishment's normal activity. Restaurants, pubs, delis, cafés and bakeries all have quiet periods when they can be happy to rent out space. Perhaps you only need a commercial kitchen one day a week, and can use it when the café or restaurant is closed.

You'd be surprised just how small and compact some commercial kitchens are. You might come away with new respect for how the chefs create so many meals in such a small space.

An added bonus is that the chef may occasionally help with cooking tips and tweaks to your recipes that help you improve your product.

Before you agree to take on any rental space, do check that the kitchen layout works for you and that the equipment is in good working order. Check it has the right utensils, too.

GETTING AROUND

Having your own transport is going to be pretty important for your business. You may need to collect from wholesalers, deliver cakes and jams to customers or attend farmers' markets with a boot-full of display equipment, an oven and a sink as well as food.

If you cannot drive or don't have a current licence, now is the time to change that.

And if you're spending a lot of time delivering, does your vehicle send out the right message? It should be clean and professional-looking, so perhaps ditch those stickers with rude or bad puns! If you own your own vehicle, cover it with signs advertising your business. Just driving around on personal errands, thousands of people will catch sight of your brand.

A car can be for both business and personal use, so consider a van or similar commercial vehicle.

All transport costs can be offset against tax – check with your accountant or local tax office for advice. If you hire a vehicle just for shows, the cost is also tax-deductible and saves you the cost of buying a vehicle. However, this is likely to be a short-term fix.

CASE STUDY
Moor Farm Shop

The Timmis and Everall families began mixed farming and breeding Hereford cattle in north Shropshire nearly 100 years ago, before combining forces in 1981 with the marriage of Mike Timmis and Hazel Everall.

An unusual wedding gift of nine Hereford cattle was the start of a business that is now managed by two sisters, Melissa and Elaine, with the support of their parents, Mike and

Hazel, and their third sister Emma. This fourth generation of Timmis have since opened a new-build farm shop on the edge of Baschurch: Moor Farm Shop.

In 2006 Moor Farm Shop opened in a single garage, adjacent to their farmhouse on the edge of Baschurch village. The next five years were spent building up a range of products and a loyal customer base.

Having outgrown the original shop space, the Timmis family expanded Moor Farm Shop to new dedicated premises. They successfully applied for grant funding from the Rural Enterprise Scheme to support the development. They were advised through the grant process by local land and estate agents. The project was completed on time and the doors opened to regular customers in 2011.

The building has been constructed with the environment in mind, with green elements including a system that utilises the hot air from the freezers and other equipment to heat the water and radiators.

In addition to expanded retail space there is now an on-site kitchen for baking bread, pies, home-cooked meals, with many more delicious sweet and savoury dishes coming soon. There is also a meat-cutting room, chilled storage and an on-site office that overlooks the retail space, so that Elaine can watch everything that is going on!

★ Moor Farm Shop | *www.moorfarmshop.co.uk*

CHAPTER 9

Recipes and Ingredients

Whatever type of food business you are running from your kitchen, it's important that you use the best ingredients. And you should be involved with a food that you enjoy eating – you'll be tasting it almost every day and talking about it with suppliers, customers and friends almost as much.

WHAT GOES IN?

The food and drink that comes out of your kitchen will only be as good as the ingredients that go into it. If you use cheap or inappropriate ingredients you will have to use magic to create saleable products.

Use the freshest ingredients, and become familiar with their typical shelf lives. Taste nuts to see whether they have turned rancid; source eggs from a trusted supplier for added flavour. And if you're baking, use fresh flour.

Be sensible about how much you spend on ingredients. Keep your customers and markets in mind when drawing up shopping lists. Don't skimp on quality, but don't scare customers away by using unnecessarily expensive ingredients.

 Constantly test your ingredients and produce to ensure your standards are kept as high as possible. While you are experimenting or developing a new product, consider keeping some for testing later – it might not taste the same after it has been sitting on a shelf for a few days or weeks.

Suppliers

Maintaining good relationships with your suppliers is an important part of any business. Whether they provide you with raw ingredients, packaging or design services, you need to be able to rely on them.

Unfortunately, some of them will let you down, so always have back-up suppliers in place. Do not rely on one source of packaging, ingredients or delivery – have a plan B for all your various suppliers.

In the meantime, keep written records of food and ingredients suppliers. Include their name and address, the type and quantity of products, and the dates when you take delivery. You may also wish to record the batch number or the 'use by' or 'best before' date. Often this information will be on the invoice, but you should make sure.

You should keep all the invoices and receipts for any products you buy from any supplier, including a shop or cash-and-carry. If there is a safety problem with food you have sold, you or an enforcement officer can then check the details of the food. Bear in mind that if a food has a long shelf life, you will need to keep the records for longer.

Make sure you choose suppliers you can trust; ask other businesses for recommendations. Before you sign up with any supplier, run through this checklist:

★ Does the supplier store, transport and pack their goods hygienically?

★ Does the supplier provide fully referenced invoices/receipts?

★ Do they have any certification or quality assurance?

* Check that the supplier has a food safety management system.

* Carry out regular delivery time, temperature and quality spot checks.

* Keep the details of your suppliers.

Your choice is important because a supplier's reliability, and the safety and quality of the food they supply, could affect your business. It is especially important that the products you buy have been stored, processed and handled safely.

Ingredients

Family, friends and customers will often ask 'what's your secret?' when they taste your food. It might be simply that you use the best, freshest and most natural ingredients – real butter, 80% cocoa-chocolate, genuine rose water rather than artificial flavouring.

It's amazing the difference that good quality ingredients can make. Chemically flavoured ice cream will never have the same taste or texture as that made with real chocolate bits, vanilla pods or freshly picked strawberries.

Of course, if you want to sell large volumes of ice cream at a music festival or agricultural show, you'll have to plan – or compromise – accordingly. So it's always worth being aware of alternatives and their relative quality.

Recipes

Ingredients
2 x Tomato
200ml single cream
100g Cheese
Basil
Garlic clove
400g Pasta

CASE STUDY
ALCHEMIST DREAMS

Chemistry graduate, artist, activist and game-maker, Ruth Ball is the creative force behind London-based drinks company Alchemist Dreams. But it wasn't until she was waiting on a grey industrial estate, for an interview for a laboratory research job in the paint industry, that she decided to make her dream a reality. Because artists "don't make house paint," she says. "They make dreams."

Ruth describes her business as: "Artisan liqueurs from the laboratory of a mad scientist". Founded in early 2011, Alchemist Dreams offers a constantly developing range of liqueurs. At the moment more than 20 are available, with at least one new flavour added every month.

You can design your own flavour or choose from popular house blends like Black(berry) Magic – a mysterious blend of blackberry, ginger and Szechuan pepper.

Ruth sells via an online shop and from market stalls dotted around London, including a monthly market in the City at Leadenhall. Weddings, corporate events such as new product launches for a cosmetic company, and hotel and restaurant openings are also a growing market for Ruth.

Ruth is enjoying the journey of creating Alchemist Dreams – within 12 months of setting up the business, she's now working on it full-time.

Although she doesn't take part in any formal networking groups, Ruth has a wide circle of friends, many self-employed in the creative industries, who have provided an informal support group. She is a member of the Experimental Food Society and is planning a number of collaborations with fellow members to develop new flavours and enticing products.

Ruth is developing cocktails to pair with cakes, and hopes to hire tea rooms in the evening to create a 'speakeasy' type atmosphere, one step away from the popular Supper Club concept.

Future market development, says Ruth, will take place at independent music and arts festivals identified as having "my type of customers and market".

TIP: "Don't be intimidated by long, complex-looking official forms. Work away at them, little by little, and they will be less daunting."

* Alchemist Dreams | *www.alchemistdreams.co.uk*
* Leadenhall Market | *www.leadenhallmarket.co.uk*

Cash and carry

The major food producers buy ingredients by the tonne, attracting discounts which you won't be able to get. You'll probably be using local farms, specialist suppliers, or wholesalers/cash-and-carry outlets such as Booker and Bestway. Armed with you business's registration number, you'll be able to 'join' a wholesaler and buy ingredients directly.

* Booker Wholesale | *www.booker.co.uk*
* Bestway Cash & Carry | *www.bestway.co.uk*

Wholesale markets

Thousand of restaurants, caterers and small food businesses buy their fresh ingredients from wholesale markets. Some open at midnight, others a few hours later. Most finish before 9am. Build up relationships with several suppliers by regularly buying from them and you will be rewarded with great advice and top quality produce.

Keep an eye out for unusual and seasonal produce – always a selling point for your products.

* **Birmingham Wholesale Markets** (*www.birmingham.gov.uk/markets*) is located in the centre of the city, supplying white and red meat, fruit, vegetables and flowers from around 4am.

* **Manchester Wholesale Market** (*www.manchester.gov.uk/markets*) is a large market in the east of the city offering fresh fruit and vegetables, and fish.

* **City Markets Glasgow** (*www.citymarketsglasgow.co.uk*) is a wholesale fruit, vegetable and flower market, and one of the largest horticultural markets in the UK, covering Scotland, the North of England and Northern Ireland.

* **New Covent Garden** (*www.newcoventgardenmarket.com*), the famous London market, opens at 3am for fruit and vegetables. Lots of wholesale catering distributors are based there, as are a few companies offering cheese, meat, fish, sandwiches, dairy and wine.

* **Smithfield Market** (*www.smithfieldmarket.com*) is a huge wholesale meat market in the City of London, where you can source any type of red meat or poultry.

★ **New Spitalfields Markets** (*www.wholesalefruitvegetableflowers.co.uk*) offers wholesale fruit, vegetable and flowers, with most produce heading for London and the Home Counties.

IN THE MARKET FOR FISH? Billingsgate (*www.billingsgate-market.org.uk*) and Grimsby (*www.grimsbyfishmarket.co.uk*) are the two biggest fresh fish markets. You can also order fish daily from companies such as Wing of St Mawes (*www.wingofstmawes.co.uk*) and Fish in a Box (*www.fishinabox.co.uk*). Check out *www.sustainablefishcity.net* for tips on sourcing fish from sustainable sources.

Organic and responsible meat

Organic food is grown to strict environmental standards that prohibit the use of artificial fertilisers and chemicals. It is often sold at higher prices than conventionally produce foods, and if sourced from the UK is generally available seasonally.

Some free-range beef and poultry farmers who aren't registered as organic still rear to high welfare and environmental standards. Their produce is known as responsible meat.

★ Soil Association | *www.soilassociation.org*

★ Meat and Livestock Commission | *www.mlc.org.uk*

★ English Beef and Sheep Meat | *www.eblex.org.uk*

★ Scottish Meat | *www.qmscotland.co.uk*

★ Welsh Beef and Lamb | *www.hccmpw.org.uk*

★ Welsh Lamb and Beef Producers | *www.wlbp.co.uk*

FOOD ALLERGIES AND INTOLERANCES

Food allergies and intolerances are increasingly common. There is a subtle difference between the two – an *allergy* produces specific symptoms, such as swelling of the lips, which usually develops within minutes of eating. An *intolerance* produces more general symptoms, such as indigestion and bloating, which can develop several hours after eating.

The most common food allergies are to nuts (usually peanuts, almonds, hazelnuts, brazil and walnuts), fish, shellfish, lactose (the sugar found naturally in milk) and cow's milk, eggs, soy products, seeds (sesame and poppy) and wheat.

Two of the most common food intolerances are to lactose and wheat.

The symptoms of a food allergy can be life-threatening, whereas the symptoms of a food intolerance, unpleasant as they may be, are never immediately life-threatening.

Allergy and intolerance checklist

★ Check your ingredients and **ensure any labels you produce carry a full list of ingredients and a warning of potential contents** that may cause a bad reaction. Your local Environmental Health Office will be able to advise you on using ingredients that could cause an allergic reaction.

★ If you are catering private events, your **host should have heard from their guests about allergies**. Check with them in advance.

★ Your **staff should be made aware of food allergies**: from the chef preparing food with cheese (milk allergies), salads (walnuts in the Waldorf) or chocolate cakes (nuts), to the waiters who might be questioned about ingredients when taking or delivering orders. The same is true of food being produced in a kitchen where traces of nuts are common.

For information on food allergies and intolerances check:

* National Health Service | *www.nhs.uk/conditions/food-allergy*

* Allergy UK | *www.allergyuk.org*

* UK government | *www.food.gov.uk/policy-advice/allergyintol*

* British Hospitality Association | *www.bha.org.uk*

* Coeliac UK | *www.coeliac.org.uk*

Emergency treatment

Never guess whether a certain dish contains particular ingredients. You and your staff *must* know. If someone has a negative reaction to eating your food at a catered event or in the market, respond calmly and professionally.

Most people with severe allergies carry portable injectable epinephrine – it is not your responsibility to carry it or administer it.

If a customer asks for emergency assistance (or if someone is finding it hard to breathe, if their lips or mouth are swollen, or if they collapse) don't hesitate:

* call 999 immediately and describe what is happening

* don't move the person; this could make them worse

★ send someone outside to wait for the ambulance and stay with your customer until help arrives.

Local council environmental health officers will advise you how to safely handle foods that can cause severe allergic reactions. St John Ambulance and the British Red Cross offer good first aid training courses.

★ St John Ambulance | *www.sja.org.uk*

★ British Red Cross | *www.redcross.org.uk*

SCALING UP PRODUCTION

Recipes developed in the home kitchen can be tricky to scale up for production in a commercial kitchen. Kirsty Gillies (see page 58) found a local baker to practise scaling up her recipes. Kirsty says:

> "What we did in the kitchen was not immediately compatible in the bakery, but by testing recipes in a commercial environment we gained an understanding of consistency of dough and how to tweak recipes. We did lots of trial bakes to ensure we created a consistent product, with the same great taste, quality and texture."

If you want to scale up, approach other small business manufacturers – speak to them, learn from them. See how you can adapt to commercial equipment, and get to understand how commercial baking or food-producing equipment works.

Scaling up production requires recipes to be adapted and tested repeatedly. Miranda Ballard, from upmarket burger company Muddy Boots, recalls that:

"Making significantly larger batches involved testing subtly different recipes and, inevitably, tweaking ingredients."

"To move from making 20 burgers to producing 200 was not simply a matter of multiplying ingredients by a factor of ten. Making significantly larger batches involved testing subtly different recipes and, inevitably, tweaking ingredients."

When scaling up a recipe, Miranda would typically keep a close eye on the seasoning and binding properties of the burger. What might the issues be with your food when moving from small to larger-scale production?

TIP: Keep a watch on quality control of your ingredients if you outsource production to a manufacturer.

QUALITY STANDARDS AND CERTIFICATION

British Retail Consortium

In 1998 the British Retail Consortium (BRC) (*www.brcglobalstandards.com*) developed and introduced the BRC Food Technical Standard to be used to evaluate manufacturers of retailers' own-brand food products. This standard is quite complex and is often used by larger food companies and those trading internationally.

SALSA

SALSA (Safe And Local Supplier Approval) (*www.salsafood.co.uk*) is a nationally recognised food safety certification scheme specifically developed for small and micro producers. It is a foot-in-the-door approval scheme, allowing producers to get their produce in front of national and regional buyers. The scheme also provides helpful guidance to members.

To gain certification, a SALSA inspector will visit your premises, spending around four hours auditing your business and checking your paperwork – for example, HACCP, training records, pest control records and process records. There are fees associated with being a SALSA member, including a £100 first-year membership fee.

Soil Association and Organic Farmers & Growers

These two groups are the largest certifiers of organic food in the UK.

They both promote organic food production and certify over 70% of all organic products sold in the country. Whether you're a farmer, a food manufacturer or a formulator, they can provide a range of useful technical information, put you in touch with buyers and suppliers and keep you up to date with the latest marketing opportunities for organic products. Both certification schemes come with logos which can be used for marketing and on packaging.

* Organic Farmers & Growers | *www.organicfarmers.org.uk*
* Soil Association | *www.soilassociation.org*

Freedom Food

Freedom Food (*www.rspca.org.uk/freedomfood*) is the RSPCA's farm assurance and food labelling scheme. It is the only UK farm assurance scheme to focus solely on improving the welfare of farm animals reared for food.

Red Tractor

You'll have seen the Red Tractor (*www.redtractor.org.uk*) symbol on many meat, dairy and vegetable products. The scheme is all about sourcing food which is safe to eat and that the animals have been well treated.

FoodLovers Britain

FoodLovers (*www.foodloversbritain.com*) is a private company run by farmers' market pioneer and food writer Henrietta Green. Many of the approved businesses "make local and regional, seasonal food a priority, be they producers, shops or cookery schools".

CHAPTER 10

Branding and Packaging

In today's crowded marketplace, your products have to stand out. What goes into them is not the only thing that's important. How you present them is vital too.

For too many start-ups, investing in design for branding and packaging is a low priority. But remember, should you ever wish to sell your business, it's really the 'brand' that you'll be selling much more than recipes or production capacity.

DESIGN APPEAL

"Using design is not just about making the things you produce look good," says the Design Council, the UK's organisation for promoting effective design. "It's about making them work efficiently and about enhancing the profitability of your business."

It's best to try and get this right as early as you can. Comprehensively re-branding further on down the line can be a fraught process. That doesn't mean you need to keep your brand absolutely set in stone from the start; but it does mean the broad features must be in place.

After that, successful branding is an ongoing act, requiring monitoring and periodic tweaks to keep things as focused as possible (at least every two or three years, recommends the Design Council).

★ Design Council | *www.designcouncil.org.uk*

★ Business Link | *tinyurl.com/businesslinkcreate*

CASE STUDY
POSH POP

Claire Martinsen, of Posh Pop-makers Breckland Orchard, got lucky through a Google search when looking for a designer. Though it wasn't all plain sailing ...

> "I met three different designers and companies. The first presented an optician's brochure she had designed – I couldn't visualise how my design would be developed or look. The second, a brand/advertising agency, wanted between £10,000 and £15,000 to develop the look and feel of the company and design.

> "Fortunately, my third meeting was with a local freelance designer who asked for payment only on completion of an accepted design and charged around £500."

Claire knew what she wanted, and had examples of other products with labelling that she liked. Critically, she had a strong sense of identity for the company that would inform the look and feel of its branding.

> "I imagined sitting in a sunlit café, being served a refreshing drink in a beautifully designed bottle ... I knew I was not just selling a drink, but an experience, a lifestyle."

You have to put yourself in your desired customers' shoes as they look at what you have to offer. What will persuade them to part with their money?

★ Breckland Orchard | *www.brecklandorchard.co.uk*

IT'S A BIT LIKE THERAPY

Visiting a designer can be rather like having therapy. "We ask lots of questions to get to know the client, product and what they are expecting to achieve," says David Myerson, from branding and packaging agency Hurricane Design (*www.hurricanedesign.com*).

He warns that it can be very disheartening to have your dreams examined so closely. But it's also invaluable. "Designers ask questions dispassionately," says Myserson. They just want to understand the genuine essence and advantages of your product. That means this is often the first time that a prospective food producer is properly tested on their idea.

Typical questions branding experts will ask include: What makes it so special or unique? What does your product promise to the consumer? Why should someone choose your product over others? What makes your product stand out from the crowd? Do you have a single point of difference or rather a combination of factors that will attract attention? Do you have a unique:

* process

* philosophy

* ingredient

* recipe

* way of doing things?

DESIGN BRIEF: A CHECKLIST

Here's a checklist of things to include in your design brief, the document that gives the designer a framework for creating your brand. It's important to build one even if you're the one who'll be doing the designing – it'll help keep the creative process on target.

Business background

Who your customers are; strengths and weaknesses of your skills; strategic objectives; competitors and their existing marketing.

Project objectives

What you want to achieve and how the design will be used.

Limitations

What constraints there are to fit the new design in with existing designs or parts; specific technical or legal requirements; manufacturing processes needed; what is inside and outside the project's scope and any environmental issues.

Creative direction

Style; materials; tone; mood; communication and usability.

Project management

Budgets; schedule and deadlines; details of the team or person liaising with the designers and managing the project and how success will be measured at the end.

Intellectual property (IP)

Establishing who will own IP rights to the designs being produced.

SOURCE: DESIGN COUNCIL

PACKAGING

Food needs packaging for several reasons – to protect and preserve its contents, provide nutritional advice, list ingredients, and advise about possible allergic reactions. Much of the information included on a label is required by law.

But packaging is perhaps also the most vital way in which a food business builds a relationship with its customers. It's the ultimate embodiment of brand.

This section will look at how to fulfil both sides of that equation successfully.

Three types of packaging

Everyone in the food chain from producer to consumer has a stake in food packaging.

The packaging you'll be most involved with is *primary packaging*: the aluminium, plastic, cardboard or paper wrapping that holds your products together, and is designed to generate interest and paying customers.

Other packaging is needed to transport your goods over long distances, often by courier or haulage companies. This is *secondary packaging*. It is more robust, and does not require fancy design. It's often made of corrugated cardboard and allows easy handling at storage depots, for example.

Legal requirements

There is a lot of information that has to be shown on packaging. You must clearly show:

* the name and a description of the product

* cooking and heating instructions

* total weight and all ingredients in descending order of weight

* date of manufacture alongside manufacturer's name and contact details

* storage instructions

★ shelf life

★ allergy information.

Any packaging in direct contact with food also has to be 'food safe', and packaging manufacturers have to comply with EU regulations. For more info, check out Trading Standards Institute (*www.tradingstandards.gov.uk*). Information about labelling legislation is also published by the Food Standards Agency (*www.food.gov.uk*). In 2014, the EU is introducing a new set of packaging rules that will become mandatory in 2016.

Standing out

Highlight your selling points

★ Use 'flashes' to highlight important elements of the product: Did you make it in your kitchen at home? If so, personalise and trade on this: e.g. *Made by Carla in her rural kitchen*, alongside a photograph of yourself – mixing bowl in hand.

★ Is the product locally produced? If so, where and by who? The more specific, the better.

★ Is your packaging recyclable? A must-mention, if so.

★ Does your product have a special flavouring ingredient? Or is it important that the product contains no dairy products, nut, gluten etc?

★ Let your customers know if there are other similar products in your range: other flavours, complementary foods or drinks that you make, and so on.

The bigger picture

★ Does your packaging differentiate your brand from the competition?

★ Does it communicate the key reasons your customer should buy your product?

★ Does it enhance emotional engagement with your brand? Is it building brand loyalty for your product and company for the long term?

Getting physical

★ Consider how your packaging will fare during stacking and shipping. It needs to be robust as well as eye-catching.

★ Be careful with the size of the packaging: is it standard sized? Will your package sit comfortably on a shelf next to other goods – in particular, the same sort of goods? Will your target shops have room for it?

★ Does your packaging shrink into the background or stand out from similar products? Is it noticeable on a crowded shelf?

Environmentally friendly packaging

If your packaging is certifiably less damaging to the environment, then let your customers know.

★ **Reusable packaging** can be cleaned and re-used. For example, glass milk bottles.

* **Recyclable packaging** is made of materials that can be used again, usually after processing. Recyclable materials include glass, metal, card and paper.

* **Biodegradable packaging** easily breaks down in the soil or the atmosphere.

TIP: A successful fudge-making company printed thousands of gift boxes to package the fudge for a contract with a regional airport. However, after a few weeks the order was cancelled. The company was left with thousands of boxes, paid for and printed with the airport's logo. The loss of this client hit cash flow, not least as so much money was tied up in packaging that now had no further use. The owner vowed to keep more control of her product and packaging design, inserting into contracts shared costs on packaging, marketing and promotional costs.

Mail order fishmongers Fish in a Box (*www.fishinabox.co.uk*) make the point in their explanation of the packaging they use:

> "Packaging has been an issue for us from day one. Basically we consider it a necessary evil that we always have to minimise and adopt an environmentally friendly solution wherever we can. We have had some success with our corn-starch soak pads and recycling the polystyrene boxes. We are now pleased to report that we have introduced an even more environmentally friendly solution to our mail order packaging. We are using an insulated foam liner made by Hydropac. These replace the polystyrene boxes and go out with a 'post-it-back' recycling bag. We hope our mail order customers like this new packaging and it will help us do our bit for the environment."

Yum, buy me!

Here are some valuable tips to take into account when creating your packaging from Carla Boulton, owner of design company Naughty Mutt (*www.naughtymutt.com*). Carla has worked with several start-up and medium-sized food producers on their design and packaging.

"
- ★ Identify your target market. Your product needs to call out to them: 'Yum, buy me!'

- ★ Commission great product photography: clear, delicious-looking images will take your product to another level.

- ★ Good design *will* sell a great product. Work with a designer to develop a beautiful brand to reach your market.

- ★ Get into the mind of the consumer. What is their ideal home like? How will your product fit in?

- ★ If the product is attractive, can you incorporate a clear window in the packaging to show it off?

- ★ Highlight the ingredients and issues that make your product different, tastier, better value, etc. "

Consistency is king

Ensure your packaging design is consistent with the rest of your branding. Brand identity needs to be prominent on all faces of the packaging. This could mean that colour is consistent throughout all faces, or that part of the logo design is extended to sides of the packaging. You must imprint your brand in the customer's mind.

If you have a range of products, make sure the packaging works together.

CASE STUDY
Gourmet Vanilla

Gourmet Vanilla is a father-and-daughter business set up to market the first vanilla pods to come out of southern India.

David and Maggy Dean have supplied top quality vanilla to leading restaurants in London and throughout the UK and Ireland since 2001. Following retirement after a career in the food industry, David helped develop the Indian vanilla industry with a focus on improving quality and marketing. Today, Gourmet Vanilla's product quality and range easily matches that of the more widely know Madagascan vanilla.

Maggy says that without working on improving quality, taste and flavour with interested chefs at the start of the business, it would have been very difficult to get product quality right for the market.

Maggy has three tips for companies putting together their brand and packaging:

1. When building your website, make sure it can be read on mobile devices like smartphones and iPads. Within a year of opening our online shop, 20% of our online orders came from mobile devices.

2. Don't underestimate the power of good quality design and packaging. At the start we were creating and printing our own labels to save money, until a buyer said the packaging, sometime reused, did not reflect the high quality of the product or what the company represented. We have also standardised the look and feel of the packaging so that retail clients, wholesalers and consumers immediately recognise the brand.

3. Distributors are very important. Increasingly chefs from chain restaurants and Michelin-starred restaurants are ordering from one distributor so that they receive just one invoice rather than dozens of suppliers sending in a confusing variety of invoices with different payment terms.

★ Gourmet Vanilla | *www.gourmetvanilla.co.uk*

CHAPTER 11

New Product Development

WHAT IS NEW PRODUCT DEVELOPMENT (OR NPD)?

The NPD process creates new food and drink products that have the best chance of succeeding with customers. This is the lifeblood of all businesses in the long run. It is key to growth and survival.

In a proper NPD process, numerous new ideas will be rejected before they reach the market. Even those that make it to market might not succeed – but they should have a better chance than most.

There are 12 key stages in the development of a new product:

1. creation of the brief
2. market research
3. design brief/design specification
4. idea generation
5. concept screening (prototyping)
6. sensory evaluation
7. commercial viability testing
8. review/modifications
9. pilot run
10. sampling the market
11. launch
12. product management.

In other words: dreaming it up, making it delicious, and getting it to market.

New products aren't only created from scratch, though. You can also try simply tweaking flavour, size, packaging or filling.

You can also try targeting your existing products at new outlets. For example, if you are selling cupcakes to parents for their children's birthday party, why not also look at how the same cupcakes can be offered to the corporate market with minimal adaptation?

CASE STUDY
ELLA'S KITCHEN

Ella's Kitchen was founded by Paul Lindley, previously a senior executive with kids' TV channel Nickelodeon. As a father of two – including a daughter called Ella, after whom his business is named – he was concerned by alarming increases in childhood obesity. He believed that if children were given healthy food choices from the beginning, this would help prevent them from developing bad habits as they grew older.

After being made redundant, he spent two years developing his company – starting with an idea for a brand before developing products to meet the brand's ideals: food children enjoy that is "tactile, looking and smelling great, and stimulating all the senses to get them to eat healthily".

When Ella's started, most baby food was sold in glass bottles and not packaged to appeal to children. "We needed to be different and innovative," said Paul. So, for example, "we bought brightly packaged, plastic pouches to the baby food market."

"Today, we take 50 new product ideas and reject 47. That's a lot of decisions, but they must be made otherwise the company will stall."

★ Ella's Kitchen | *www.ellaskitchen.co.uk*

FROM IDEA TO NEW PRODUCT

Development starts with market research – ask yourself, is this a product that you want or that the market wants? If it's a pet project for you, then you're going to have to work harder to get your customers to buy it.

Once you've got the idea, do the sums. Will you need to buy different, more expensive ingredients; is new equipment necessary; what are your margins and profits – is it viable? Does it fit comfortably into your existing product range – or are you branching out into new and less certain territory, which might end up being a distraction?

Consider what the product will look and feel like:

★ size

★ shape

★ shelf-life

★ weight

★ sensory characteristics (taste, texture, appearance, etc.)

★ costs

★ ingredients (with quantities).

And then test your best ideas. South Devon Chilli Farm undertook NPD at its farmers' market stall. Co-founder Steve Waters says: "We came up with jams and sauce recipes and watched closely to see which flavours people sampled and enjoyed most."

"It's always very useful to see what customers go for before entering production."

Two of the most important food trends of recent times are seasonal and ethical foods. Both are well worth considering when trying to develop new products.

'TIS THE SEASON

With a bit of forward planning, there are plenty of products that can be offered with a seasonal dimension – from seasonal bread to seasonal chocolate. Many people now credit seasonal food with fuller flavour and more authentic links with farmers and producers. Keeping an eye on what's available seasonally might also inspire you to adapt your offerings creatively throughout the year.

Another benefit of using seasonal produce is that an overabundance in a recent harvest will reduce prices.

Winter

One of the busiest seasons for the food and catering businesses, the winter season could well be your most profitable period. Red-letter days include Christmas, New Year's and

Valentine's Day – not forgetting celebrations that flourish in some areas thanks to influence from America, including Thanksgiving (fourth Thursday in November) and Halloween (31 October).

Many winter foods can be made well in advance. Christmas staples such as plum or sloe gin, mincemeat for mince-pies, fruitcakes, chutneys, piccalilli and other hamper must-haves can be made weeks or even months in advance. Make sure the products are stored safely and containers are clearly labelled.

Chocolates, heart-shaped cakes, and other romantic foods such as oysters and caviar require preparation a little closer to sale – but it may be worth securing ingredients in advance, taking delivery when you finally need them.

Spring

Spring is a popular time for weddings. It also offers catering opportunities for Mother's Day (fourth Sunday of Lent); Father's Day (third Sunday in June); and St Patrick's Day (March 17).

Stock up on green food colouring for St Patrick's Day, an increasingly popular celebration, even amongst those with no obvious connection to Ireland. Think Irish soda bread, green-iced cupcakes or Guinness beef stew.

Eggs and creatively presented chocolates are obviously popular gifts at Easter, and there is always demand for inventive, beautiful takes on such products, e.g. cloth-wrapped, silk-ribboned single eggs.

Summer

As summer fruits can now be harvested, it's a great time to sell them freshly picked at farmers' markets or to turn your attention towards lighter puddings and snacks. Summer is also barbecue season, and that means everything from organic sausages to homemade ketchup and mustard.

Weddings come thick and fast in the summer months; a vital market for caterers, and even suppliers specialising in certain foods.

Use summer colours for inspiration when putting together your products. You may also find more exotic flavours such as rose, jasmine, ginger and fennel to be popular.

Autumn

Autumn is when so many fruit and vegetables are picked, cooked, pickled and enjoyed, not least at harvest festivals. Apples and pears are at their peak, while pumpkins and squashes are in demand for Halloween parties.

Pumpkins are incredibly versatile and photogenic. Caterers can add pumpkin soup to the menu, and toasting pumpkins seeds, perhaps with a sprinkling of sea salt or curry powder, is a simple and delicious way to use by-products from pumpkin carving. The truly versatile muffin is an ideal end-product for the pumpkin flesh.

In the diary ...

* **National Farmhouse Breakfast Week** (*www.shakeupyourwakeup.com*) – January

* **Burns Night** (*www.scotland.org*) – 25 January

* **Chinese New Year** – January/ February

* **Valentine's Day** — 14 February

* **National Chip Week** (*www.potato.org.uk*) – February

* **Fairtrade Fortnight** (*www.fairtrade.org.uk*) – February/March

* **British Pie Week** (*www.britishpieweek.co.uk*) – March

* **Shrove Tuesday** – March

* **St Patrick's Day** — 17 March

* *Country Living* **Spring Fair** (*www.countrylivingfair.com/spring*) – March

* **Mother's Day** — March/April

* **Easter Sunday** — March/April

* **British Sandwich Week** (*www.sandwich.org.uk*) – May

* **National Vegetarian Week** – May

* **Harvest** — September

* **National Cupcake Week** (*www.nationalcupcakeweek.co.uk*) – September

* **British Food Fortnight** (*www.lovebritishfood.co.uk*) – September/October

* **British Cheese Week** (*www.britishcheese.com*) – September/ October

* **Chocolate Week** (*www.chocolateweek.co.uk*) – October

* **National Curry Week** (*www.curriesonline.co.uk*) – October

* **Halloween** – 31 October

* **Bonfire Night** – 5 November

* **National Taste of Game Fortnight** – November

* *Country Living* **Christmas Fair** (*www.countrylivingfair.com/xmas*) – November

* **Christmas Day** – 25 December

* **Boxing Day** – 26 December

TIP: Don't forget less regular cultural events, which can always be a useful focus for new products or product variations. Keep an eye on local and national sports teams/events, college graduation dates, one-off public holidays, etc.

Eating seasonably

Eat Seasonably (*www.eatseasonably.co.uk*) is a charity celebrating eating fruit and vegetables when they're at their best. It is supported by various groups including the National Trust, the RSPB and the Women's Institute.

Celebrity chefs such as Hugh Fearnley-Whittingstall and Gordon Ramsay have highlighted the benefits of seasonal food – including better taste and texture.

As well as fresher, more authentic food, serving what's seasonal also results in another distinctive story your business can tell about itself.

Top tips from Eat Seasonably

*   ★ Consider offering weekly or monthly specials based around what's in season.

*   ★ Talk to your suppliers and look out for gluts – buying in season is often cheaper.

*   ★ Use a seasonal logo on menus to highlight seasonal choices.

*   ★ Get your staff involved in talking about the benefits of eating seasonably.

*   ★ Use the changing calendar and notable dates to create events that get your customers involved.

ETHICAL EATING

Are you working directly with suppliers in the developing world – perhaps sourcing tea, coffee or spices?

It's a handy selling point, as well as something that can give focus to your ideas as you develop new products. (Not to mention being, of course, a good deed towards those suppliers.)

Trumpers Tea, for instance, buys tea from across southeast Asia and South Africa. Owner Claire Trumper is "passionate about working within the Fairtrade system wherever possible":

"We frequently travel to the beautiful and outstanding countries of origin and work with the producers to learn more about their communities and the families that are directly affected by the sale of tea."

Ethical trading involves responsibility for the labour and human rights practices within a company's supply chain.

As part of your marketing/charity work you might work with a local group such as Concern Universal on local fund- and profile-raising events.

Contact these groups if you source ingredients from the developing world and, in Fairtrade's words, wish to encourage "better prices, decent working conditions, local sustainability, and fair terms of trade for farmers and workers in the developing world".

* Fairtrade Foundation | *www.fairtrade.org.uk*

* Ethical Trading Initiative | *www.ethicaltrade.org*

* Concern Universal | *www.concernuniversal.org*

* Trumpers Tea | *www.trumperstea.co.uk*

PART
THREE

Marketing and Sales

CHAPTER 12

Promoting Your Products

S o your food business is planned, registered and running. Your products are delicious, profitable and beautifully packaged, and your product range is growing.

But all this will avail you nothing if no one has heard about you. That's where promotion comes in.

IMPRESS THE PRESS

Getting your products or business mentioned in the press can really boost sales. But remember that press can be good or bad. If your product is not of consistently good quality, press will only hurt you. Before you begin any public relations campaign, you should make sure your products are good value and your management and operations are in order.

That being sorted, good mediums for exposure include the following:

* industry and trade publications

* business journals

* local newspapers

* regional magazines

* blogs and journals

* local radio stations

* local television stations.

Attract interest in your story and company by building a relationship with the journalists and news media relevant to your product. Put together a list of magazines and relevant writers who you're going to target. Be selective, and sparing, in the number of times you get in touch.

And when you do get in touch, make sure there's a story there. Ways to create a story include:

* Host or sponsor events: tastings, competitions, charity fundraisers, concerts. (Make sure you invite the media in advance, or take photos and supply them afterwards.)

* Donate to charity: give a portion of your sales to a local charity or host a fundraiser.

* Make creative changes: noteworthy changes to packaging, ingredients.

* Put on a publicity stunt: cook your sausages in fancy dress in the street.

* Offer to write a story or give a recipe to a local paper or magazine.

How to write an effective press release

PR is about key messages being repeated so that they stick in your customers' minds. Ad hoc efforts are understandable, but to make a proper impact it is best to plan for the long term, says Greg Simpson of Press For Attention.

Keep it simple

People worry that their efforts don't sound flashy enough to warrant attention but you aren't aiming for a Booker Prize – you're aiming for coherent and interesting *news*.

This is crucial. If the story isn't new then it just isn't news and falls at the first hurdle.

Structure

Use "Who, What, When, How and Why?" as a framework and imagine yourself as the journalist. Is this definitely of interest to their readers? Is it simple enough to understand? Does it stand up on its own?

I would stick to 300 words maximum and try to be even more brief if possible. Keep the press release focused on the story/news angle. Don't be tempted to waffle about the business in general or about the way it is run unless that is the angle.

You can add all of the 'about us' stuff in an editors' notes section after the press release with your captioned photos.

Hit them between the eyes

Journalists get hundreds of press releases every day and are not going to scan through trying to find something of relevance. I prefer to call the journalist beforehand to outline my story and refine it for their audience. This helps iron out any creases and demonstrates that you are trying to work with them and with their audience in mind.

Don't be tempted to start hassling

Some PRs will disagree but never chase a journalist once you have sent it. If it is good enough, they will use it. Hassling will not push it to the top of the pile and may see it heading towards the recycle bin. Be patient and able to help if the journalist does come back. Don't go on holiday the day after you have sent a story out.

Hooked on news

If you do lack news, all is not lost. You may be able to find a hook by providing relevant insight or commentary on a current trend or topic. Ever wonder why familiar faces crop up in features in magazines or on the radio? It is because they are ready and reliable sources of interesting and relevant comment.

Build a relationship

PR is not a 'them v. us' war with journalists. It's a working relationship where both parties stand to gain. They get insight and/or news, you get free publicity in exchange for a fresh take on things or for your role in illustrating an issue.

New Mail

TIP: Remember, always keep it simple and keep it relevant!

★ Press For Attention | *www.pressforattention.com*

COMPETITIONS AND PROMOTIONS

Competitions or simple promotions are a great way of grabbing a potential customer's attention and getting them to try your product. They are also popular with local magazines and newspapers, whose editors may be looking for prizes or reader deals.

You can also run competitions from your market stall, or in the online world via your website, Facebook and Twitter.

The legal bits

Both competitions and promotions involve legal obligations. If you are working with a magazine, they will have a strict policy to follow. As a rule of thumb, they should be honest and truthful; there is a responsibility not to mislead the shopper by inaccuracy, ambiguity, exaggeration or omission.

If you use the term 'free' in your marketing, ensure that there are no hidden costs that the prize winner has to pay.

"If you use the term 'free' in your marketing, ensure that there are no hidden costs."

CASE STUDY
HIGHLAND GAME

Scottish food producer Highland Game successfully used a range of marketing techniques to engage with consumers and help them discover the benefits of venison when it was still a young company.

A cookbook titled *The Name of the Game* was published and an advertising campaign run in *Country Living* Magazine, while cookery demonstrations were staged at the *Good Housekeeping* Institute in London.

This activity has been supported by Highland Game's cookery roadshows and its venison masterclasses, which have been staged in AGA shops and at country fairs and trade exhibitions.

* AGA | *www.agaliving.com*

* *Country Living* | *www.countryliving.co.uk*

* *Good Housekeeping* Institute | *www.goodhousekeeping.co.uk*

* Highland Game | *www.highlandgame.com*

AWARDS

If you win a food award, spread the word and get it on your packaging as soon as possible.

Keep the details fresh, though. If you are still promoting an award won ten years previously, people may ask why you haven't won anything since.

To find about upcoming awards, visit *www.awardsintelligence.co.uk* or check out the following:

National awards

The Guild of Fine Food (*www.finefoodworld.co.uk*) is the UK trade association for anyone making or selling local, regional and speciality food and drink. Their Great Taste Award is widely seen as a mark of excellence. If you win you can use the logo on your packaging, marketing and press releases.

The *Country Living* Magazine Kitchen Table Talent of the Year Award (*www.kitchentabletalent.com*) is ideal for people setting up a business based on home-grown skills; from baking and craft to gardening and home design. The prize will include profile in the magazine and advice/support from business experts.

The Food and Farming Awards (*www.bbc.co.uk/foodawards*) is a very prestigious scheme run by the BBC's influential weekly *Food Programme* on Radio 4.

The British Street Food Awards (*www.britishstreetfood.co.uk*) were set up in 2010 to recognise the best of the 10,000 businesses who sell their products on UK streets.

The *Observer* **Food Monthly awards** (*www.guardian.co.uk/observer-food-monthly-awards*) are high-profile awards run by Sunday newspaper the *Observer*.

The Quality Food Awards (*www.qualityfoodawards.com*) focus on products on sale in UK grocery outlets. A special category exists for 'Local Food', with reduced entry fees.

Free From Food Awards (*www.freefromfoodawards.co.uk*) celebrate the innovation and imagination shown by the food industry in creating foods that do not include one or more of the ingredients: wheat, gluten, dairy products, eggs, yeast, soya, sugar, etc.

The *Grocer* Own Label Food & Drink Awards (*www.thegrocerfoodanddrinkawards.co.uk*) is an award scheme run by the industry magazine the *Grocer*.

The Soil Association Organic Food Awards (*www.soilassociation.org/awards*) celebrate the best in organic food and drink.

The World's Original Marmalade Awards (*www.marmaladeawards.com*) are a fun and popular celebration of the best in marmalade.

Local awards

Here are just some of the many local awards run by local newspapers, county magazines and county councils:

* Taste of the West | *www.tasteofthewest.co.uk*

* Sussex Food & Drink Awards | *www.sussexfoodawards.biz*

* Flavours of Herefordshire | *www.visitherefordshire.co.uk*

* Cumbria Life Food & Drink Awards | *www.cumbrialifefoodawards.co.uk*

* Wales the True Taste Awards | *www.truetaste.tv*

* Grampian Food Forum Innovation Awards |
  www.aberdeenshire.gov.uk/foodawards

* Scottish Excellence Awards | *www.scotlandfoodanddrink.org*

NETWORKING

Networking is one of the best promotional tools available and can be done for free or for a small fee.

You can even join groups that meet for breakfast (very early mornings!), lunch or dinner.

Networking can put you in contact with potential customers, suppliers, mentors and business friends. You can also pick up local knowledge about new markets, shop and café openings and suchlike.

You need you to choose which networking groups you attend carefully – will you meet the right type of people and businesses who can give your business a helping hand?

Before you attend the first meeting of a network club, be sure to check whether you will be asked to give a quick 60-second presentation about your company. If so prepare your 'elevator pitch' (see page 15).

Ensure that you not only hand out your business cards, but also collect those from others. Then, when back in your home office, send an email or telephone those whose companies are most relevant. Begin to build business relationships. If you are proactive in following up such meetings, you never know where it will lead!

Check out your local group at sites such as Find Networking Events (*www.findnetworkingevents.com*). Try Meetup (*www.meetup.com*), Ecademy (*www.ecademy.com*) and Facebook (*www.facebook.com*) for networking groups and events. Check out Smarta's event listings at *www.smarta.com*.

* Business Networking (International) | *www.bni.eu/uk*

* Young Entrepreneurs | *www.yesnetwork.co.uk*

* The Food Network | *www.thefoodnetwork.co.uk*

CASE STUDY
MORE TO LIFE THAN SHOES

More To Life Than Shoes is a national network, "offering group mentoring, master classes and inspiration for working girls and budding female entrepreneurs."

It's run by two friends, Emily Nash and Nadia Finer, who set up the group to attract women who were thinking of starting a business or a career change and wanted to meet like-minded women. As Emily says:

"We wanted that support network, which is something you don't always get from family and friends because they're sick of hearing about it."

Like many networking group, MTLTS groups offer regular meet-ups which bring "members together to get motivated, share cool new ideas, collaborate and take steps towards their goals."

So what was their inspiration? Nadia and Emily say they wanted to love what they did for a living, not loathe it. They wanted to make a change, but they didn't know where to go for inspiration and advice. So they set off on a mission to find the country's coolest women (from foodies to neuroscientists, biologists to builders, and entrepreneurs to engineers), corner them and pump them for advice to find out exactly how they made their dreams come true.

"This is the perfect time for women to take control in their careers, despite the recession, redundancy threats, pay gaps and rising childcare costs. Our book *More To Life Than Shoes* is a call to action to women everywhere to find their spark, crank up their confidence and blaze a trail out of the doom and gloom to success."

★ More To Life Than Shoes | *www.moretolifethanshoes.com*

CASE STUDY
A TASTY MARKETING MAILOUT

" Stephanie Salo is a professional photographer, specialising in food – which works out well, as she loves to cook! When she received an adorable mini-spatula in the mail, she was inspired to create her own equally memorable marketing mail-out package.

To let people know that she's available for all their food photography needs, Stephanie decided her marketing mail-out would have the theme 'Home made goodness' – and that meant including some bespoke recipe cards made from MOO Postcards. "After looking through many of my cookbooks, nothing seemed to fit. So I came up with six of my best photos and made 'Recipes for Satisfied Clients' on postcards instead.

"Although not edible, it expressed my creative side and working style. This was important since the promo was being sent to art directors and photography editors, and the majority of them were seeing my name and work for the first time," says Stephanie.

Putting her money – or in this case – her baking skills where her mouth is, Stephanie made batches of home made cookies to go with the postcard, her own logo-stamped mini spatulas, and sealed each cute brown box with a MOO logo sticker.

And the tagline? "I dare you to eat just one!" Now that's a tasty bit of marketing!

SOURCE: MOO.COM

★ Stephanie Salo Photography | *www.lensandladle.com*

CHAPTER 13

Your Business Website

ONLINE PRESENCE

Your online presence is like a shopfront. If you don't have one, many (perhaps most) of your potential customers will never know you exist. And that's true whether you're aiming at a local, national or global market.

You can either have your website built to your own requirements, or invest in a template design that you then tweak.

Find a designer

★ Elance | *www.elance.com*

★ Design Council | *www.designcouncil.org.uk*

★ Design Week | *www.designweek.co.uk*

TIP: Draw on your branding design brief (see page 154) to put together an effective brief for your web designer.

Find a template

★ Moonfruit | *www.moonfruit.com*

★ Create | *www.create.net*

★ Magneto | *www.magentocommerce.com*

Buy a domain

* 1&1 | *www.1and1.co.uk*

* 123-reg | *www.123-reg.co.uk*

* Easily.co.uk | *www.easily.co.uk*

"Small companies can act quicker, can use social media more effectively to, for example, recognise and spot trends."

– Paul Lindley, *www.ellaskitchen.co.uk*

PAGES TO INCLUDE

Think of your website as a brochure for your products. Here are the pages that it really can't be without ...

About us

Tell your customers about your business concept and values, as well as a little bit about your background.

Simon Wicks, editor of Enterprise Nation (*www.enterprisenation.com*), says it can be easy to overlook what your customers will find interesting.

"There's a story that weaves its way through every tale you might have to tell. I call this the story of the telling detail. It's that small but significant aspect of what you do that creates a genuine sense of curiosity about what you do and how you do it. It's very easy to overlook because you may just take it for granted. I'll give you an example. While interviewing Victoria Clair of The Castle Cakery (*www.thecastlecakery.co.uk*), she mentioned – almost in passing – that she exports cupcakes to France. This was completely normal to her, but I was bowled over.

'You *export* cupcakes? To *France*, the home of patisserie?' I spluttered. 'They don't have cupcakes in France,' she replied matter-of-factly. 'But you *export* cupcakes? *How?*'

Every business has stories to tell, and they're all interesting – if you understand what's going to spark the interest of your audience and you tell the story with the right focus.

So what's your story?"

News

Show off any awards and good reviews you receive. And keep customers informed of where they can buy your products – for example at which farmers' markets you'll be attending, shops that stock your items, etc.

TIP: Make sure that competitions, promotions and new releases that you offer in the real world are promoted across your online presence.

Products or services

List food and menu items with ingredients and pricing. Consider creating pdfs or printable documents of recipes and menu suggestions featuring your products.

FAQs

Frequently Asked Questions, allows you to pre-empt enquiries from potential and existing customers such as: Are your products organic? What is the shelf life of your products? Where can I buy your food?

Contact us

Email newsletters

Email is one of the most cost-effective ways to let your customers know what you're up to. Building up a database of email addresses allows you publicise new products, competitions and promotions (e.g. 10% off at the next market with a token attached to the email) to all those who are interested at the click of a button.

You can send e-newsletters out as often as you wish, although any more than one a week is likely to annoy your customers. MailChimp (*www.mailchimp.com*) and Constant Contact (*www.constantcontact.com*) are popular platforms for managing and sending out mass emails. They're free to set up; charges only begin once you start sending out a certain number per month.

TIP: Remember, you cannot add addresses to your marketing database without getting the receiver's permission.

Promotional emails are read more on weekends when people have more free time, although there is some evidence that emails sent on Wednesdays are opened most often.

The legal bits

TAKE CARE OF THE TS AND CS: When building your site, include some basic terms and conditions. These will cover information about the site content and your policy on data privacy. View sample T&Cs on the Business Link website: *bit.ly/csYSTz*

ATTRACTING VISITORS

The good news is that attracting visitors to your site is not just about how much money you throw at marketing. A targeted approach with a little creative thinking can take you a long way.

Nick Kington, managing director of e-commerce supplier Actinic (*www.actinic.co.uk*), shares his tips for drawing visitors to your site on a budget:

1. Get seen in search engines

Search engines are the number-one source of new visitors to websites and Google is by far the most popular. Search engines present their results based on the sites considered optimal for the words or phrases entered.

Use tools such as the Google Keyword Tool or WordTracker (*www.wordtracker.com*) to help decide which keywords or phrases are best for your business. Many e-commerce software suppliers provide tools to assist in optimising your site around the chosen keywords.

2. Experiment with pay-per-click advertising

A popular and quick way of promoting your site is to use pay-per-click (PPC) advertising services such as Google AdWords and Facebook with its demographic targeting.

Costs will depend on the keywords relating to your site and products, but you should be able to test a campaign for a low outlay. It goes without saying that you should advertise on the key phrases that you have identified.

3. Use social networks

Social networking sites such as Facebook and Twitter now provide a low/no cost way to promote yourself and your site. Facebook in particular has tools to help businesses to promote themselves. But first research which social sites your customers frequent and get familiar with how they work.

4. Don't forget email marketing

Once your database grows, use email marketing to communicate with your customers. Better still, if you have an existing customer database, use that. Email is best used for promoting special offers which can be triggered simply by clicking a link in the email.

5. Check how you're doing

However smart you are with your marketing, you can always improve. It's amazing what you can learn from tools such as Google Analytics. And it's free to use. It can tell you where visitors came from, what device they used, what keywords they typed, and much, much more. **/)**

SOURCE: ENTERPRISE NATION

TIP: Don't forget to include your URL on your packaging and promotional flyers, banners, menu boards, etc.

E-COMMERCE TOOLS

* GroovyCart | *www.groovycart.co.uk*

* Zen Cart | *www.zen-cart.com*

* RomanCart | *www.romancart.com*

* Frooition | *www.frooition.com* (shopping cart and full website)

* PayPal | *www.paypal.co.uk*

* Google Checkout | *checkout.google.co.uk*

* Sage Pay | *www.sagepay.com*

CHAPTER 14

Using Social Media

BLOGGING

Blogging about food is an excellent way of showing off your expertise and promoting your food. Doing it well is something of an art form. Jan Minihane of online marketing consultancy The Net Advantage (*www.thenetadvantage.co.uk*) offers these tips for successful blogging ...

Post title

* **Keep your title short and snappy** – make it easy for people to make a decision whether they want to read a post.

* **Fill it with keywords** – each post title needs relevant keywords in it for SEO purposes (but don't force it).

* **Ensure it's attention-grabbing** – what kind of title would make you click on a blog post? Perhaps there's a particularly powerful phrase or sentence in the post that you can use.

EFFECTIVE TITLES: e.g. 'Twitter is dead in the water', '10 Top Tips to efficient energy use', 'Has retail shopping had its day?', 'Five guaranteed ways to boost your bottom line!'

Content

* **Keep the language simple** – write like a young teenager will be reading it. Make it a conversation.

* **Lead paragraph** – needs to be the attention-grabbing bit, especially if the post is quite long. Grab your readers' attention with a summary of what they will read, or pose some questions that the post may go on to answer.

* **Calls to action** – ask questions. It make people think of an answer, and therefore more likely to leave comments. Ending a post on a question, if possible, is particularly good.

* **Not too long** – the overall length of your posts should ideally be 300 to 500 words. Keep your sentences short to hold your readers' attention.

* **Keyword rich** – if you want a particular segment of your audience to read it, make sure you have specific keywords (e.g. bake, ingredient, farmers' market) included so it's easier for them to find the post.

"Make it a conversation."

* **Sign off the post** – e.g. 'that's all for now folks', 'next post coming soon', 'TTFN'. This makes it more intimate and conversational than just finishing with a sentence. It's critical to sign off with your name when more than one person will be contributing to the blog, as different styles can confuse readers.

* **Internal links** – Use links to other pages of your website. Link to other relevant blog posts or another relevant page. Where do you want your reader to go?

★ **External links** – Use links to external websites (and where relevant let that site know you have linked to them – they may help you promote your blog if you've given them a positive mention). But keep it genuine!

★ **Add videos** – media-rich blog posts are more interesting to look at and hold visitors' attention for longer.

★ **Don't sit on the fence** – bland is boring in the blogging world. If you're going to give your opinion on something, commit to it – you want to get a reaction (good or bad).

★ **Write with passion** – if you can't get passionate about your product, service, or industry, how on earth are you going to maintain readers' attention?

★ **Review your post** – draft it in Word, spell- and grammar-check it – nothing looks worse than a blog post with a mistake in!

★ **Get personal** – if you are your brand, your blog will be partly about you. Don't be afraid to add your own experiences. You'll often find the best response when you admit you got something wrong or are struggling with something.

Blogging platforms

★ Blogger | *www.blogger.com*

★ LiveJournal | *www.livejournal.com*

★ Tumblr | *www.tumblr.com*

★ WordPress | *www.wordpress.com*

More blogging tips and tricks

★ Become A Blogger | *www.becomeablogger.com*

★ Copyblogger | *www.copyblogger.com*

Food blogging groups

★ UK Food Bloggers Association | *www.ukfba.co.uk*

★ Midlands Food Bloggers | *midsfoodbloggers.wordpress.com*

★ Food Blogger Connect | *www.foodbloggerconnect.com*

CASE STUDY
THE FOODIE BUGLE

Silvana created online magazine *The Foodie Bugle* (*www.thefoodiebugle.com*) because she "wanted an online presence that was not focused on celebrities, passing fads and advertising."

> "I have been a cook and cookery teacher all my life and had bought and read probably every other cookery, food, wine and travel magazine and book ever published."

So her idea crystallised into a collaborative magazine where passionate food and drink bloggers, reviewers and writers could all join to celebrate the very talented artisans all over the world that work to put excellent produce on our table.

In addition, contributors could write about all the issues bubbling around the world of food and drink, from interviews with cookbook writers to research about new farm shops and essays about family kitchen heritage. *The Foodie Bugle* embraces both creative writing and factual research.

Silvana says the early days were tough:

> "I worked day and night: writing articles, travelling to interviews, setting up our social media presence, marketing the magazine, finding writers, commissioning photographers and so on. I did all of it with my own money. *The Foodie Bugle* takes no advertising revenues and has no financial sponsorship".

To raise money for the website, Silvana has launched a series of paid-for *Foodie Bugle* lectures based in Southrop, Gloucestershire.

Silvana's key tips

1. Be prepared for nothing to happen overnight. Development of *The Foodie Bugle* has been an organic, gradual process.

2. Be prepared to work really hard, consistently. When you are a blogger there are no days off. You're in a global marketplace.

3. Go for gold: there is too much rubbish on the internet already. Do everything you can to produce really good, unique, well written and beautifully photographed work.

4. Follow the truly talented people and hopefully they will follow you back. **/ /**

* *The Foodie Bugle* | *www.thefoodiebugle.com*
* Moresoda [web designers for the magazine] | *www.moresoda.co.uk*

Food writers

Thousands of amateur food blogs are now available, covering just about every subject. Vanessa Kimbell's blog (*www.goddessonabudget.co.uk*) has climbed to the top of an extremely competitive market.

> "Few people can make a living from blogging, so I have a number of income streams, including advertising on the blog, endorsing products, writing newspaper columns and books," says Vanessa.

Her book, *Prepped*, is described as "an original and cleverly thought-out book aimed at … 'time-short foodies', offering simple recipes with complex flavours." Vanessa also has a regular spot on BBC Radio Northampton.

Bristol-based Genevieve Taylor (*genevievetaylor.blogspot.com*) is another accomplished blogger. She has established herself as a successful food stylist and photographer, and is the author of *Stew*. She says catering at home can take over your house, but writing and blogging fits in well with childcare.

Genevieve spent three days on a course with BRAVE (*www.brave.org.uk*), a local business-support group that advised on the practicalities of setting up a business. Her first thoughts were to set up an outside catering business, but through working on a business plan she realised that her talents lay elsewhere.

Keep in touch

Keep in touch with the food industry with these leading industry websites:

* *The Grocer* | *www.thegrocer.co.uk*

* *Caterer and Hotelkeeper* magazine | *www.caterersearch.com*

* BBC *Good Food* magazine | *www.bbc.goodfood.com*

* *Delicious* magazine | *www.deliciousmagazine.co.uk*

* Food & Drink Federation | *www.fdf.org.uk*

* National Farmers' Retail & Markets Association | *www.farma.org.uk*

* F3 Consultants | *www.localfood.org.uk*

* BigBarn | *www.bigbarn.co.uk*

TWITTER

Twitter (*www.twitter.com*) is an internet phenomenon, and one increasingly used by all types of business to keep in contact with customers. It's a must for your food business.

Twitter is all about communicating in short, sharp bursts of 140 characters or fewer. You can add photos as well, and it's free to use.

If you see a phrase such as @brightwordpub or @e_nation in a tweet, these are just other tweeters 'handles'. You can tweet to them by including this handle in a tweet of your own.

"Chewing gum while chopping onions helps stop you from crying."
— a tweet from chewing-gum makers Peppersmith (*www.peppersmith.co.uk*)

Tweet like a pro

Mark Shaw (*@markshaw*), author of *Twitter Your Business*, says that successful business tweeters are those who divide their tweets equally between chit-chat, sharing information/resources and demonstrating expertise.

Social chit-chat

Sharing news and information of a personal nature does not mean that you have to give away your inside leg measurement. Only tweet about what you are comfortable with.

Also, try to ask others what they are up to and get a conversation going. Conversation is what Twitter is all about.It is an excellent way to break down barriers and to start a business relationship.

Over time people will get to know you better and start to like you, find you interesting, and possibly become great advocates for you, even referring you to others.

Sharing information,

The information that you share can be your own material or another person's that you have found: ideas, resources, tools, websites, news and more. If you hear or learn something that you think is of interest to others, then tweet about it.

As mentioned, retweeting other people's information is really important.

The point of sharing information is that over time you can become known as the go-to person on a particular area. You want to be regarded as someone who helps others, is not selfish, looks out for others, and so on. Most people like to do business with those types of people.

Demonstrating your knowledge and expertise

You demonstrate your knowledge and expertise by answering questions and becoming a great resource for information on a certain area, and it's exactly the same on Twitter. This is your chance to really shine within your own expertise area.

This way you are helping people but not selling to them. When they arrive at your site, if they are interested in signing up to your newsletter or if they opt to purchase from your site then all the better. All you have done is educate them and not sell to them.

Be engaged

Food blogger Silvana de Soissons of *The Foodie Bugle* (@thefoodiebugle) says that above all social media is best used to be passionate and interesting about what you do.

> "Twitter and Facebook are two fantastic, low-cost, easy ways to post-as-you-go and to give people an insight into you, your values and your product. Vicky Smith of Jamsmith (@jamsmithclub), an artisan jam producer in the Yorkshire Dales, tweets photos of her foraging trips, the changing Dales weather and the process of her jam being made. These pictures give followers a real sense of her and her values, and help build trust in her as a good producer. For an internet-based business, with no PR or marketing budget, this sort of interaction with the public is invaluable."

Show who you are and the person behind the brand, says Silvana. "Find your own voice. Do not ape other people's styles. Anyone following Amelia Rope (@ameliarope), the artisan chocolate maker on Twitter, will very quickly get a sense of the ups and downs, the trials and tribulations of a start-up chocolatier's business. Amelia's voice is very vivid and very likeable."

FACEBOOK

With over 845 million users, Facebook is the most popular social networking site in the world. As every individual on Facebook has a profile, so every business should have a Facebook page: a place where people connect with your business and where you can share your latest news, photos, products, offers and more.

To create a page, head to *www.facebook.com/page*.

Post regular content and interact with your page's fans and you'll soon be thriving.

TIP: Check out the free and friendly guide to maximising your Facebook presence by Enterprise Nation: *www.enterprisenation.com/facebook-book-offer*

Advertising on Facebook

Facebook also lets you reach out to new fans through phenomenally precise targeted advertising. You can select an audience based on location, age, sex and interests, and reach out with offers, highlighted posts, posts that users' friends have liked and more.

Friends or meat?

At the beginning of 2009, Burger King launched its "Whopper Sacrifice" viral marketing campaign. The fast food chain created an application on their Facebook page that gave users a coupon for a free Whopper if they dropped ten friends from their social network.

The campaign generated an incredible amount of free press coverage. 233,906 friends were dropped in exchange for a free Whopper. Although the campaign was later suspended due to complaints from Facebook, even this controversy earned Burger King press coverage.

LINKEDIN

LinkedIn is a social network group for professionals with members in over 200 countries. Visit *www.linkedin.com*, create an account and start connecting with contacts and finding new ones. Form LinkedIn groups around your particular interest, and share knowledge, contacts and ideas.

It's a free service, although you can upgrade to a business account.

VIDEO

It's never been easier to film, edit and upload video onto your website. Using tools such as Windows Movie Maker (for PCs) and iMovie (for Macs) you can share cooking techniques and recipes with visitors across the world.

Visitors to foodie websites generally spend more time watching videos than any other online activity.

YouTube (*www.youtube.com*) is the world's most popular online video community, with hundreds of hours of video uploaded every day. Start your own business channel for free, and upload videos profiling you and your work.

CHAPTER 15

From Farm Shops to Supermarkets

W here is the best place to sell your products? What suits your products – and what suits your target customers? It could be a weekly market, a local village shop, a regional chain, a national supermarket. One, some, or all of these.

This chapter will cover pitching your products to everyone from the local farm to a globally trading supermarket group. The next will go into more detail on the slightly different challenges of front-line sales at events such as farmers' markets.

LOCAL RETAILERS

When you approach a local retailer, come armed with responses to typical questions they will have, and practise your answers beforehand to gain confidence. You want to show the buyer that you mean business.

Local pitch checklist

* Background and purpose of your company

* Take a sample for the buyer to try

* Why local produce and markets are important to you

* Do you have any promotional material to support your products: posters, recipe cards?

* Are you prepared to do in-store sampling or cookery demonstrations?

* Do you have other outlets selling your produce?

* Can you offer a range of size options, shelf lives, recommended retail prices?

* How often can you deliver? Can you restock quickly?

* Do the prices you are quoting include VAT?

TIP: As well as farm shops and cafés, make contact with local tourist attractions, B&Bs, pubs and hotels. Be creative.

Below is an adapted set of questions sent to producers from The Real Food Store, a café and bakery in Exeter, Devon. Some shops will look for more information, others less.

Whether the shop proprietor wants this information by email, on the phone or perhaps when you first enter the shop and introduce yourself, you'll need to know it. Have the answers at your fingertips:

Questionnaire

1. Name of business

   * Contact name   * Address   * Email   * Phone   * Website

2. Description of your business

3. What products would you be able to supply? (List or attach a complete product list, together with wholesale prices.)

4. What is your unique selling point? (Why do you think we should sell your produce?)

5. What is the personal story behind your business?

6. Please tell us your terms and conditions for supply – including:

    a) any minimum quantities for order

    b) order lead time

    c) frequency of delivery to our Paris Street store

    d) payment terms

7. Describe how you minimise the environmental impacts of your business? E.g. packaging.

8. If you use raw materials, where do you source these? Please list your main suppliers.

9. Do you have public and product liability insurance? (Please note you will be required to present us with a copy.)

10. If relevant, how do you ensure the highest standards of animal welfare in your business or are you registered with any recognised organisations, e.g RSPCA, etc.

11. Are you organically certified? (Again – we would need to see the certificate.)

12. Please tell us anything else you consider relevant (membership of food and drink associations, awards, etc.).

13. Do you have photographic material we can use?

★ The Real Food Store, Exeter | *www.realfoodexeter.co.uk*

Always research the company or shop you're hoping will list your products. If possible, talk to other suppliers selling products (that don't directly compete with you!) to understand how the shop interacts with its suppliers.

Country Markets

For more than 90 years, a network of Country Markets has been selling homemade baked goods, preserves and home-grown fruit, vegetables and plants across England and Wales. Joining this organisation may be your route to the local market.

Country Markets is a cooperative social enterprise with about 12,000 members, aiming to "promote diverse and delicious local food to the public". It "prides itself on the quality of its products and for keeping traditions alive, as well as creating friendly shopping environments."

Members are called 'Country Markets Cooks' and sell their products through local retail outlets such as community and village shops, farm shops and garden centres, as well as local Country Markets.

Country Markets provides training, information and education services for its producers. It researches and passes on news of developments from DEFRA, Trading Standards Officers, environmental health officers and other regulatory bodies. As a Country Markets producer selling through retail outlets, you will be supported by a business support advisor in establishing your business.

CASE STUDY
ELAINE, A COUNTRY MARKETS COOK

Joining Country Markets enabled Elaine to give up her day job and make a living doing what she loves: cooking!

Elaine started by selling preserves to use up a glut of apples, and now produces savoury dishes, especially game pies and casseroles, and unusual preserves for two Country Markets in South Yorkshire. Her speciality jellies are sold into local shops.

Elaine's husband is a gun-dog trainer and has permission to pick from the hedgerows. His foraging also finds its way into Elaine's tasty preserves.

> "Everyone in Country Markets is very supportive. I enjoy the camaraderie of it all, meeting people who have lots of talent and have the time to talk and share," says Elaine.

★ Country Markets | *www.country-markets.co.uk*

Food hubs

There are numerous food hubs that promote personal contact between producers and shoppers. Some have a physical building which acts as a focus for community activities around food, while others focus on providing a local distribution service for producers and consumers.

Some also process local food and provide cooked meals for the public sector or provide workspaces for small producers.

Making Local Food Work is working with several such hubs to help them become more sustainable and economically viable.

* Bodnant Welsh Food | *www.bodnant-welshfood.co.uk*

* Ludlow Food Centre | *www.ludlowfoodcentre.co.uk*

* Making Local Food Work | *www.makinglocalfoodwork.co.uk*

* Sustain | *www.sustainweb.org*

* Transition Network | *www.transitionnetwork.org*

CASE STUDY

SCOOP, YORK UNIVERSITY

Scoop provides students at York University with the opportunity to purchase ethical, local food at affordable prices. It is a non-profit organisation run by students for students, offering good food at cost price.

To find out how to set up a food co-op in a college or university, check out *www.foodcoops.org*.

UNICORN GROCERY

Since opening in 1996, Unicorn Grocery has offered a wide range of local, organic, fairly traded and wholesome food to its South Manchester customer base. Unicorn has become one of the largest and most successful whole food outlets in the UK, and was named Best Independent Shop by the *Observer Food Monthly* and Best Local Food Retailer (2008) by Radio 4's *Food Programme*.

Find out more at *www.unicorn-grocery.co.uk*.

Pitching to restaurants

Say you're selling cheese to a restaurant. You need to inform the chef and waiting staff about its provenance; how it's made; which wine or biscuits it complements. Create a story around your food.

You must sell it to the buyer for the restaurant who must 'sell' it to the chef, who then must put it on the menu and sell it to the waiting staff who must sell it to the diner.

If waiting staff can't pronounce the food then it comes off the menu pretty quickly.

'Local' marketing

Shropshire Granola (*www.shropshiregranola.co.uk*) is a great example of how to incorporate local sourcing in marketing, going as far as thanking "the honeybee for the sweetness of our cereal".

Based in Bridgnorth, Shrosphire, the company has a section on its website called 'Our Shropshire', listing local foodie events and giving customers the opportunity to record their memories of the county and share photos.

The company believes "in the importance of location" – and that's why "all our flavours are locally sourced. We believe in nature and nurture and understand the benefits of living in one of Britain's most rural counties."

Information is provided on the website's TLC section about ingredients' taste and flavours, where they are sourced, and various health benefits they bring. "Each mouthful of my granola had to be a tasty representation of Shropshire," says Alexandra Anderson, company founder and managing director.

REGIONAL AND NATIONAL RETAILERS

Perhaps you're happy supplying your customers at farmers' markets or food festivals – but what if you set your sights on the shelves of a supermarket chain?

There are regional and national chains; Booths of northwest England on the one hand, for example, and Waitrose, Sainsbury's, Asda, etc. on the other. This section will look at how to sell your products into them effectively.

Many national chains, multiples and supermarkets encourage small producers to contact them. If you are a member of a regional food group, then use their expertise when planning your approach. Groups such as Tastes of Anglia and Food & Drink from the South East regularly host 'Meet the Buyer' events in which producers are introduced to buyers from a range of stores, including the major supermarket chains.

The Waitrose supermarket group has published a 'Small Producers Charter' that describes their policy towards developing working relationships with potential suppliers.

The company believes that:

> "the future of British food depends upon long-term, positive contact between supplier and retailer ... The Waitrose Small Producers Charter demonstrates that you can get

trust, commitment and support from a supermarket. If you don't like what you see you can walk away. But we want to hear from people with good food to sell – and we want to taste what they have to offer."

Supermarket chain Sainsbury's has promised to double the amount of British food it sells by 2020, as described in its '20 by 20 Sustainability Plan'. While much of this effort will be aimed at the larger farms and food producers, it is keen to introduce more regional and local products to its stores.

One route to get your produce on Sainsbury's shelves is via its Supply Something New Programme, launched in 2010, with a website (*www.supplysomethingnew.co.uk*) through which UK food producers can contact the company directly.

If you are selling baked goods – e.g. muffins, gingerbread, gluten-free cakes – consider other types of foodie chains such as coffee shops (Starbucks, Costa Coffee, etc.). These also offer opportunities for local, niche products.

Waitrose's criteria for what constitutes local food are quite strict. Does your produce meet their demands?

* Locally produced food will be supplied to branches within a 30-mile radius of production.

* You will not be wholly dependent on Waitrose as a primary customer.

* Products from local suppliers will most likely be delivered direct to branch; any alternative distribution route will be arranged with the full agreement of that supplier.

* The foods will most likely be made by small craft producers (employing less than 10 full-time staff) but may come from a suitable medium-sized supplier (employing up to 250 staff).

★ Waitrose already sells distinctive quality foods with provenance and integrity. The recipe should ideally have provenance or tradition in the area and 'wave the flag' for the locality.

★ Recipe/further processed foods will be made with the best quality ingredients, where possible sourced from the area (for example, in a clotted cream ice cream from Cornwall, the clotted cream and eggs should also be sourced from the same county).

★ Ingredients should be simple and recognisable – not a list of chemical additives, such as stabilisers, emulsifiers, preservatives, etc.

★ Organoleptically [taste, sight, smell, touch], the foods should be at least as good as if not better than a Waitrose own label equivalent (if there is one). The exemplary taste will come from the quality of ingredients combined from [sic] the very best in preparation and cooking skills.

★ The producer will have strong links with the local economy. ''

Asda has a comprehensive policy about sourcing local foods and becoming a 'local' supplier (*www.asdasupplier.com*). The company now offers 3,000 regional lines with products local to each of its stores and deliveries made to local food hubs. As the company says:

> "We won't take a sausage, call it a local sausage and sell it across all our stores; we have a different sausage for each region."

Market research company IGD has identified three key reasons shoppers give for buying local food. These attributes can be used in your marketing efforts and business plans:

((
* Freshness – over half (57%) of shoppers perceive local food to be fresher because it hasn't travelled as far.

* Economic factors – over half (54%) want to support local producers, while many others see it as a way of supporting local retailers (34%) or keeping jobs in the area (29%).

* Environmental factors – three in ten (30%) shoppers are motivated to buy local food because they think it is good for the environment because it hasn't travelled as far.
))

Foot in the door

Before approaching any supermarket, make sure you do thorough market research. Buyers representing your potential client will expect you to know plenty about the company and its existing products. They will also expect you to know every facet of your own business – from where ingredients are sourced and production methods, to your accounts and target market.

Talk to experts in your regional food group. They've seen it all before. They can also put you in touch with other local producers who have experience of selling into supermarkets.

Consider your costs and pricing policy carefully. You may be expected to contribute to marketing; for example, part funding special offers, two-for-one offers and simple price reductions.

If your ambition is to move on from supplying local clients to a supermarket, the buyers will want to be absolutely sure that, if necessary, you can supply tens, maybe hundreds of shops with your product at a consistently high standard, and deliveries will be made on time, that your supply chain is robust and that you have the necessary infrastructure and support in place. Your products will need barcodes and you should be able to accept and respond to orders via email.

Be prepared for honest appraisal of your product, its tastes and flavour, and packaging. It's rare that a supermarket will take your product on first sight. They might ask for changes to packaging, so that your product stands out on crowded shelves.

PITCH TIPS FOR MEETING SUPERMARKET BUYERS

Here are some top tips for going into that all-important pitch meeting.

* **Be clear and concise.** What are you offering? What do you want? Make sure your focus is clear.

* **Pitch in layman's terms.** Not that supermarket buyers are laymen. But you have to remember that, for all their expertise, no one can be as well acquainted with your product as you. Don't treat them like idiots, but don't be overly technical – remember that they must always consider the customer's point of view, and customers are rarely persuaded by technical benefits over practical benefits.

* **Include robust sales forecasts and profit projections.** Your pitch will be redundant without them. Remain ambitious, but – and this is fundamental – realistic.

* **Know your finances** from top to bottom. Nothing annoys buyers more than a sloppy grasp of the numbers.

* **Practice makes perfect:** prepare with family and friends who can offer honest, critical feedback in advance.

* **Find out how much time you have** for your presentation, and practise to that timescale. Don't rush. Pace yourself.

* **Are you unnecessarily repeating yourself,** or giving inconsequential information? Don't!

* If you've already sold your product to other parties, **let the panel know**.

* Laptops, screens and similar equipment may be available, but **rehearse your presentation without using them in case they aren't** – or in case they stop working halfway through.

* Use props, distribute handouts, but **make sure they actually add something** to your pitch.

* **Try not to fidget.** It's a common display of nerves and will distract your audience.

* **Don't forget to smile.** It may be daunting, but pitching should also be fun in its own way.

BOX SCHEMES AND ONLINE STORES

Box schemes may be able to include some of your produce on a seasonal basis.

There's a huge variety of box schemes out there: some are run by local farms selling just meat products, while others have national distribution. Customers who register with a scheme get a weekly delivery of assorted produce delivered to their front door.

Contents vary widely depending on the seasons. Scheme operators will often be able to help shift your produce if you're unexpectedly stuck with a glut of, say, soft fruit. Companies such as Abel & Cole and Riverford run country-wide schemes. More local ones are typified by Growing Communities in Hackney, North East London, a flagship project of the local food movement.

CASE STUDY
GROWING COMMUNITIES

Growing Communities is a financially independent community-led organisation based in Hackney, North East London.

Over the past ten years it has created two main community-led trading outlets – an organic fruit and vegetable box scheme (now packing over 1,000 boxes a week) and the Stoke Newington Farmers' Market, the only weekly all-organic farmers' market in the UK.

Both aim to harness the collective buying power of the community and direct it towards farmers who are producing food in a sustainable way.

* Abel & Cole | *www.abelandcole.co.uk*

* Riverford | *www.riverford.co.uk*

* Growing Communities | *www.growingcommunities.org*

CHAPTER 16

Selling at Events

S elling your products at events is an important route to market: from weekly farmers' markets to events such as the *Country Living* spring and Christmas fairs.

Before the event, always tell people you're going and where they can find you. At the event, it's a question of being clear on your offer, attracting people to the stand with giveaways or tasty refreshments, and collecting data so you can follow up with potential customers after the event and keep improving your products.

Oh, and wear comfy shoes!

FARMERS' MARKETS

What makes a proper farmers' market? According to FoodLovers Britain it's where:

★ "Everything on sale is grown, reared or processed by the stallholders themselves.

★ "The stall is run by the farmer, grower or processor (or members of their team) so they can answer your questions."

Reducing food miles – the distance food has travelled in being transported from where it is grown and produced to where it is sold – is a key motivator behind farmers' markets.

Farmers' Weekly magazine ran a popular campaign in 2006, 'Local Food is Miles Better', based in part on the growing desire of consumers to reduce food miles, support farmers and keep jobs in the countryside (as well as enjoy fresher produce).

The distance a stallholder can travel to attend a farmers' market is often restricted – usually to no more than 30 miles or within the same county; or, in London, to within 100 miles of the M25.

Online farmers' markets are also beginning to build a following amongst suppliers and consumers. You simply pay a small commission to the website in exchange for listing your produce. You can also access produce from farms themselves through organisations such as Farm Direct and Virtual Farmers' Market.

* BigBarn | *www.bigbarn.co.uk*

* Farm Direct | *www.farm-direct.com*

* Virtual Farmers' Market | *www.vfmuk.com*

It's important that your products are the right fit for farmers' markets. Do they:

* help bridge the gap between community and countryside?

* reduce food miles by being locally produced/processed?

* have extra freshness and taste and help to highlight the seasons?

* cut out middlemen and shorten the supply chain, meaning you can keep more of your takings?

TIP: *Buying* from a farmers' market allows you to build your relationship with your suppliers in person, allowing you to shop with confidence.

Market data

Tish Dockerty, of tdky Consulting, researched farmers' markets in Shropshire and pinpointed some key points for producer and stallholders.

" ★ Farmers' markets serve the needs of the local communities first (69% from within five miles) but also draw people into town from a wider area (15% from between five and 15 miles).

★ A significant number of customers interviewed were holiday makers or on a day out (17%).

★ Customers like shopping at farmers' markets because they like to support local producers.

★ Customers value the quality of produce on offer at farmers' markets.

★ Farmers' market customers are very loyal.

★ Customers spend between £11 and £50 at farmers' markets and on average spend more at larger markets. "

FOOD FESTIVALS

Food festivals are now a regular fixture in the UK's social calendar. They're also one of the most important ways in which the public get to know about new foods and drinks.

What do they involve?

Festivals feature everything from cookery displays and demonstrations, to specialty food markets, chef competitions, artisan making 'n' baking workshops and educational lectures.

Unlike regular high street shops, retailers at food festivals also offer samples – giving customers the chance to taste before buying and hopefully becoming a loyal customer.

A common theme is celebrating the range and quality of local foods. Some festivals are focused on a particular dish or ingredient, such as the Newlyn Fish Festival in Cornwall or the Chilli Fiesta in West Sussex.

Often they host a parallel beer, cider or wine festival.

Who puts them together?

Food festivals are hosted by many different groups, organisations and companies. They can be found in a huge variety of places, from city centres to castle grounds and garden centres.

How can I get involved – and is it worth it?

If you want buy a pitch at a show, you'll need to book early. The better-established events often open bookings as soon as an event closes, selling out months before the next event opens.

Whatever products you're selling, it's unlikely that you'll face overwhelming, direct competition. Most well-run, reputable shows will not sell more than three or four pitches or stall spaces to companies selling the same sort of product.

Renting a stall is a straightforward process. Organisers will generally have a booking form and welcome pack. The pack will lay out details about charges and costs; when you can set up your stall and 'tear down' at the close; the type of public liability insurance you'll need; power supplies, waste disposal, parking, and what equipment is included. Most ask stallholders to bring their own chilled cabinets, fridges and freezers, hobs and other equipment.

Stallholders are likely to be asked to complete a risk assessment form, considering all potentially hazardous aspects of your business (tripping and slipping, or using gas cylinders for cooking), and what risk management plans you have in place to mitigate or manage such issues.

A welcome pack might include such valuable information as where the organisers are planning to market the event and how you can link your website to the festival's own site.

Where to find your local food festival:

* VisitBritain | *www.visitbritain.com*

* FoodLovers Britain | *www.foodloversbritain.com/foodevents*

* Love British Food | *www.lovebritishfood.co.uk*

* Visit England | *www.visitengland.com*

* Discover Northern Ireland | *www.discovernorthernireland.com*

* Visit Scotland | *www.visitscotland.co.uk*

* Visit Wales | *www.visitwales.co.uk*

FARMERS' MARKET AND FESTIVAL KIT LIST

Before the event

* Fuel for car/van

* Tyres pumped

* Directions to location

* Food ordered and delivered

* Equipment cleaned and in working order

TIP: You usually have 90 minutes set-up time. Fellow stallholders are often happy to lend you stuff forgotten at home when setting up in the early hours of the day. However, it's better to be organised; it'll boost your reputation amongst your fellow sellers.

Display and catering

★ Gazebo/open tent (if not supplied by organiser)

★ Table and table coverings

★ Display items (shelving, glass cases, doilies, props)

★ Product signs and labels (wipe, boards – see *www.chalkboardsuk.co.uk* – and pens, chalk)

★ Price signs

★ Stationery – marking pens, tape, scissors, tape, pencils, paper

★ Water spray (to keep fruit and veg looking fresh)

★ Fridge, oven, stove, gas

★ Electrical extension lead(s)

★ Lighting

★ Giveaways. If you're feeling generous you could give little promotional items such as pens, badges or coasters, to high spending customers. Check out Promofix (*www.promofix.com*) for examples.

Sales and marketing

* Cash float

* Credit/debit card machine (if using)

* Receipt pad

* Calculator

* Marketing literature

* Business cards

* Paperwork/bowl for collecting email addresses

* Recipe cards (gives people ideas for how to use your products and keeps your name in front of them)

* Scales

* Spare batteries

Supplies

* Disposable gloves

* Aprons

* Paper/plastic bags

* Knife or serving utensils

* Trolley

TIP: When offering samples or selling high value products from a market stall – for example, paté or cheese – use a very sharp knife and a catering-standard cutting board to avoid creating crumbs or similarly small pieces that cannot be sold. Margins can be very tight and wastage from poor slicing can wipe out profits.

Product-specific supplies

★ Bakery boxes

★ Plastic wrap (for cheese, meats)

★ Cocktail sticks for samples

Personal comfort

★ Warm clothing

★ Wet weather protection

★ Drinks and food (coolbox in summer)

★ Chair

★ Carpet/cardboard (to stand on)

★ Comfy shoes

★ Mobile phone (fully charged)

Cleaning supplies

* Handwash and hand sanitiser

* First-aid kit, with blue plasters

* Tissues, towels, paper towels and cloths

* Rubbish bags

* Cleaning fluids, bleach

* Broom and dustpan

RUNNING A SUCCESSFUL STALL

Here are the four major components of running a successful stall at events.

1. Build a story around your food

* Explain your products – fresh, seasonal, local, special variety, regional food

* Talk about how you grow, rear, make what you are selling

* Tell people why what you do is good for the environment – organic, animal welfare, less sprays and pesticides

* Remind people that they are supporting the local economy

* Tell people if you use less packaging

* Solve problems by telling them how to use/cook/store your produce

* Give them recipe ideas to inspire them

* Point out other items on the market that might complement what you are selling

* Offer something to keep them going until the next market – freezer packs

2. Make customers your most enthusiastic fans

* Get to know your regulars by name and greet them

* Invite customers back: 'See you at the next market'

* Give them what they want – do you know what that is?

* Consider pack sizes, price breaks, variety packs, gift wrapping

* Run your own unofficial loyalty scheme

3. Make your stall inviting – tempt people to stop

* Add theatre to your stall – cook or prepare something even if it's just bunching radishes

* Have samples available

* Be friendly, be factual, be helpful, have fun – if you look as though you're having a good time, your customers will respond positively. Try to include customers in any conversations you are having.

* Put products in the customer's hand – they'll almost always buy

4. Handling complaints

* The most helpful customer is one that tells you when they are unhappy with something.

* The least helpful is one that doesn't tell you but tells ten friends that they didn't like your product and/or the market.

"Word of mouth is the most effective marketing tool for your business and the market – and it's free."

– **Country Markets**

It's vital you make the most of your time at events. Claire Martinsen of Posh Pop producer Breckland Orchard shares her top tips for the big day ...

" Arrive early

Leave plenty of time to get there and to get set up. Generally the earlier you arrive the closer you will be able to park to your stand or area. There can also be unforeseen problems in getting there, and starting the day feeling flustered is never a great feeling.

Dress your stand

It's no good having the most amazing-tasting food without it being presented brilliantly too. Over time you'll get quicker at setting up your stand, learning what goes best where and what displays are most effective in attracting attention and sales. If you're offering samples of your produce, make sure there are enough available, that you can safely dispose of waste such as napkins and cocktail sticks (used to sample sausages and olives, for example).

Bunting is colourful, fun and attracts attention. You can make your own using bondaweb and old tea-towels, or choose from a huge variety in the shops. A pull-up or PVC banner, emblazoned with your company name and attractive photographs, creates interest and can advertise your company to passersby.

Presentation

Both your products and the people behind the stall need to be well presented. Wear an apron, it's like an unofficial uniform and is closely associated with the kitchen. Wear a name badge, too. It breaks down barriers, puts your customers at ease and encourages conversation.

Keep warm

It will always be colder than you think, so dress in layers and make sure you take lots with you. Feet can get freezing standing still on concrete or tarmac, and if that happens then a square of carpet is amazingly helpful – failing that, a couple of layers of cardboard really does help.

Pack your own food

Take food and drink with you for lunch and snacks. It saves time, money and hassle. You'll likely be serving people during peak eating hours, so taking time off to go and get lunch from elsewhere just may not be possible.

Packaging

When people buy a well-known food brand, they buy into all that the brand promises. With an unknown or small-scale product, those brand promises are simply not known – thus the people selling the product are almost as important as the product itself.

Think about how you dress, what you wear and your overall appearance. Don't let the product down by not thinking it all through.

"Successful food entrepreneurs recognise that branding, image, presentation, perception are as important, sometimes more important than the food itself."

– Olga Astaniotis, The Olive Grows

Pricing

Don't hide the pricing away – have it on clear view to everyone coming to the stand. At the end of the day, you have products to sell, and you need to tell customers how much they cost. People will often give your products a miss if they see they have to ask how much they cost – no one likes the idea of having to then politely decline to purchase if the price doesn't meet their expectations.

Cash and change

Go to the bank the day before and get a stash of change. Tailor your change to your pricing. If your products cost £3.50, you are going to need lots of 50ps and £1 coins but probably not that many 20p/5ps. If all else fails you can possibly get some change from other stallholders, but it's better to be organised.

Sampling

Sampling is one of the best sales tools that you have. If you are just starting out, then you need to think about how you are going to sample and what additional equipment you'll need. For example, for drinks, Breckland Orchard uses 2cl sampling cups.

Food buyers can be reluctant to try something new, particularly if they are introducing it to a fussy family. Allowing them to taste and chatting with them about the product is a great way to break down barriers and overcome fears about wasting money and not actually liking the product when they get home.

Sampling should be a little theatrical – a colourful display and perhaps you and your team wearing special aprons or similarly distinctive clothes to draw attention to your offerings. It works well when you're introducing a new product or flavour into the market. But don't ever stop: there will always be someone who hasn't tried your products.

TIP: Share recipes and ways to use your products with potential customers. If you're selling jam or honey, you don't need to tell them how to spread it on crumpets, so offer unusual and interesting uses and ideas for your product, such as a bakewell tart, nougat or salad dressings. If you're selling artisan bread, hand your customers a recipe for homemade croutons and they may go home with an extra loaf.

List of stockists

If customers love one of your products, they'll want to know where they can buy them in future. Going equipped with a list of stockists or a website of where to re-order will enable customers to repurchase down the line.

Engage with your customers

It's true, people buy from people! The people on your stand are key in engaging with people, at being a real champion of the food they are selling. Days can be long and it's essential to keep up the energy and the conversation throughout the day.

At food festivals and farmers' markets it should be a pleasure for customers to buy from you.

Market research

Try out new recipes, colours, shapes, flavours, tastes or products. People browsing markets are drawn to stalls with energy and innovation. Talk to opinionated foodies in attendance to find out what's working and what's not, then test changes at the next market. Don't take negative comments personally. Keep minor niggles in proportion.

Set a target and evaluate

Don't be so desperate to get sales that you lose sight of costs. Take into account everything like labour, travel, stand costs, waste, samples, etc.

Do a quick evaluation afterwards – what went well, what didn't go so well, what stock/varieties sold, what can you do differently next time? Then be really harsh about whether the event is right for you.

It takes time to build up clientele at a farmers' market, so give it at least six weeks. But equally, if things aren't working out then try something new – don't keep repeating the same mistakes.

Stock up

If you've set realistic targets, an optimum stock level should follow. It's nice to run out of stock, but not halfway through the event – that just means lost sales that you could have made. Similarly, if your products are fresh, you don't want to be taking home lots of leftovers. It takes time to get this absolutely right.

★ Posh Pop, Breckland Orchard | *www.brecklandorchard.co.uk*

TIP: Breckland Orchard sells many different flavours of non-alcoholic Posh Pop from their website but only takes a small selection to markets. "Too much choice can put off customers, but I do keep a few bottles of our other flavours under the table for regular customers."

CASE STUDY
The Lawn

A regular festival and outdoor show visitor, Mel Capper was fed up with burgers and chips and stewed tea being the food of choice at so many outdoor events. This frustration led her to set up her business, The Lawn, with the aim of offering high-quality produce at outdoor events, preferably using locally sourced ingredients and sold at a reasonable price.

Mel's idea focused on catering in warmer summer months and supplying specialist teas and blends throughout out the year to generate year-round income.

She warns that, with the outside catering market being so weather-dependent, it's very difficult to forecast income. Having products that are less reliant on sunshine helps immensely with cash flow. Of course, their range of loose-leaf tea can be sold at summer events as well, so there also isn't too much jumping around in production.

The company also runs a bespoke mobile teashop offering drinks and classic English picnic food and cakes.

What about the future?

"We plan to build the business by increasing our internet and wholesale income for the tea, and by taking part in a greater number of events as we gain experience. We're also aiming for more events that invite us, so avoiding high attendance fees. Further products for our collection will follow to help build our brand as well."

Mel's top five things she wished she knew before going into business

1. It will take six months longer than you think it will before you are ready to trade.

2. Setting up the business can easily cost more than you anticipate. Mine cost 20% more than my top-end estimate.

3. Even though people tell you it will and you won't want to believe them, setting up a business really does dominate all your free time and thoughts for at least a year.

4. It's important not to try to do too much too soon.

5. The right mentor can give a tremendous boost to a start-up business.

★ The Lawn | *www.thelawncollection.com*

"A farmers' market is more than a collection of individual stalls, it is a retail entity. You have a collective responsibility for the success of the market."

– **Country Markets**

The highs and the lows

After many hours of preparing for and attending food fairs and festivals, Miranda Ballard of Muddy Boots shares her experience of the potential highs and lows of selling at events.

What can go wrong

* Make sure signage is large enough to be seen and read, and robust enough to withstand wind and rain.

* Proofread all literature very, very carefully and get other people to double-check spellings, especially of names, dates, web addresses and contact details.

* Get the relevant insurance – food, venue, technical equipment.

* Ensure your marketing message is simple, clear and concise. Keep your language direct and simple.

* You might be lucky to break even on the first event, but consider it great PR, a learning exercise – enjoy the fact that your brand is growing and that you went out and 'did it'.

Getting it right

* Find a format that suits you. Consider other events and learn from your own experience of attending events.

★ Local endorsement of an event is useful and gives it kudos and respectability.

★ Take photos, videos, get quotes from customers – all this can be used to promote the next event.

★ Involve other local suppliers; they will spread the word. Sales of your product will be boosted in the days and weeks after the event in local outlets, impressing your shop/deli customers.

★ Muddy Boots | *www.muddybootsfoods.co.uk*

Conclusion

I hope you have enjoyed reading this guide and that it helps you to create a great food business that uses all your skills and love for food. As you will have seen, there's lots to get cracking on with. There's also a great deal of support out there. Use it.

Local and regional food groups and Business Link are typical of the organisations waiting to offer help. Their knowledge will be a great help in developing both the technical and creative sides of your business.

The most important step on any journey is the first. It's time to get started. I wish you every success.

Bruce McMichael

Links

Who to tell

Local council: Your kitchen must be registered as health and safety checked by your local council. Contact them to arrange an inspection visit.

* *www.direct.gov.uk*

HMRC (HM Revenue & Customs): HMRC handle tax matters for the government. If you use an accountant, they can help you navigate through the UK's tax maze.

* *www.hmrc.gov.uk*

Useful government links

Food Standards Agency: Information and guidelines on hygiene regulations

* *www.food.gov.uk*

Health and Safety Executive: Advice about health and safety regulations

* *www.hse.gov.uk*

Trading Standards Institute: Outlines laws concerning trading standards

* *www.tradingstandards.gov.uk*

Farmers' markets, real and virtual

Farmers' markets: Display your produce at farmers' markets. First you will need to contact the environmental health officer at your local council to get approval.

★ *www.farma.org.uk*

BigBarn: A community interest-owned website where you can source local, seasonal, organic and sustainably grown food.

★ *www.bigbarn.co.uk*

Tastia: A food and drink site for small producers to sell products. No listing or joining fee, but a 15% commission on sales.

★ *www.tastia.com*

Virtual Farmers' Market: If you'd rather stay in the warm and sell goods from your home office as opposed to the town square, log on and sign up to the Virtual Farmers' Market.

★ *www.vfmuk.com*

Business support

Business Link: Huge online library of business advice and services from marketing and sales to accounts and legislation.

★ *www.businesslink.gov.uk*

Enterprise Nation: Friendly, informal and useful advice for small and medium sized businesses. Active social networking groups offer great support and advice.

★ *www.enterprisenation.com*

FSB (Federation of Small Businesses): Membership-based group working on behalf of the self employed and small business sector.

* *www.fsb.org.uk*

British Chambers of Commerce: Supports UK businesses looking to export

* *www.britishchambers.org.uk*

Market Research Society: Useful source of information about the value of market research

* *www.marketresearch.org.uk*

Plunkett Foundation: Helps rural communities through community-ownership to take control of the issues affecting them.

* *www.plunkett.co.uk*

Making Local Food Work: Great organisation promoting actively promoting growing and using local food.

* *www.makinglocalfoodwork.co.uk*

Startup Britain: Startup Britain is a national campaign to inspire, accelerate and celebrate entrepreneurship within the UK, with the full support of the Government.

* *www.startupbritain.org*

Smarta: An entrepreneur-led support and is backed by some of the UK's top entrepreneurs.

* *www.smarta.com*

Startups: Startups offer help and advice on starting a business.

* *www.startups.co.uk*

Live/Work Network: Experts and consultants on home-based business.

★ *www.liveworknet.com*

Country Land & Business Association: Organisation for owners of land, property and businesses in rural England and Wales.

★ *www.cla.org.uk*

WIRE (Women in Rural Enterprise): National group for women setting up businesses in the countryside.

★ *www.wireuk.org*

WFU: The Women's Food and Farming Union

★ *www.wfu.org.uk*

UK National Statistics: Census and other stats gathered by the government. Useful for market research.

★ *www.statistics.gov.uk*

Country Markets: Country Markets is a membership-based co-operative social enterprise working throughout England, Wales and the Channel Islands. Very supportive of start-up businesses, organises food, plants and craft markets.

★ *www.country-markets.co.uk*

Guild of Fine Food: Organises the Great Taste Awards, the national benchmark for the speciality food and drink sector and communicates to retailers, producers and suppliers through the 'industry voice', *Fine Food Digest* magazine.

★ *www.finefoodworld.co.uk*

Raising finance

Department for Environment, Food and Rural Affairs: Rural development grant schemes.

* *www.defra.gov.uk*

NFU Mutual: Finances for farm-related ventures.

* *www.nfumutual.co.uk/farming*

The Prince's Trust: Offers help to people ages 18–30 through loans, grants and mentors.

* *www.princes-trust.org.uk*

Triodos Bank: Finances projects with social and environmental benefits.

* *www.triodos.co.uk*

Networking groups

* More to Life than Shoes | *www.moretolifethanshoes.com*
* Business Networking (International) | *www.bni.eu/uk*
* Young Entrepreneurs | *www.yesnetwork.co.uk*
* The Food Network | *www.thefoodnetwork.co.uk*
* Find Networking Events | *www.findnetworkingevents.com*

Peers

Join in and support your fellow home-business start-ups by taking part in active forums and business owner communities. Dive in and support each other.

* Business Zone | *www.businesszone.co.uk*

* Start Up Donut | *www.startupdonut.co.uk*

* *Business Matters* magazine | *www.bmmagazine.co.uk*

* In a Fishbowl | *www.inafishbowl.com*

* Enterprise Nation | *www.enterprisenation.com*

Trade magazines

Many of these magazines have useful websites, and free, informative email newsletters.

Caterer and Hotelkeeper: Weekly magazine covering all aspects of the industry

* *www.caterersearch.com*

Food Manufacture: For the food processing industry

* *www.foodmanufacture.co.uk*

Fq, Food Quarter: Food and drink from the north east of England

* *www.fq-magazine.co.uk*

The Grocer: Food industry news

* *www.thegrocer.co.uk*

Kennedy's Confection & Kennedy's Confection Trade Buyer: Industry news, lots about chocolate

* *www.kennedysconfection.com*

Scottish Grocer: All about the trade in Scotland

* *www.peeblesmedia.com*

Specialty Food Magazine: Useful for news about the fine food market

* *www.specialtyfoodmagazine.com*

Cake Craft & Decoration Magazine: Monthly magazine for cake decorating and sugarcraft

* *www.cake-craft.com*

Cakes & Sugarcraft: Cake decoration projects and ideas

★ *www.squires-shop.com*

Wedding Cakes: Keep up with the latest trends in wedding cake design

★ *www.squires-shop.com*

Consumer magazines for inspiration and recipes

Find these magazines in your local newsagent. Useful for recipe ideas, trend-watching and potentially marketing your products.

Country Living **Magazine:** The complete country lifestyle magazine

★ *www.countryliving.co.uk*

Country Living **Magazine Fairs, Spring and Christmas:** Popular events that bring together hundreds of exhibitors from across the UK in an extravaganza of quality.

★ *www.countrylivingfair.com*

Delicious Magazine: Packed with new recipes

★ *www.deliciousmagazine.co.uk*

Food & Travel **magazine:** A guide to the world of gourmet travel

★ *www.foodandtravel.com*

Fork **magazine:** Regional food magazine, focused on the west of England and the Cotswolds

★ *www.forkmagazine.com*

Great British Food: Local food from all over the country

★ *www.greatbritishfoodmagazine.com*

Regional food and drink groups

★ English Food & Drink Alliance | *www.englishfoodanddrinkalliance.co.uk*

★ deliciouslyorkshire | *www.deliciouslyorkshire.co.uk*

★ Heart of England Fine Foods (HEFF) | *www.heff.co.uk*

★ East Midlands Fine Foods | *www.foodanddrinkforum.co.uk*

★ Taste North East | *www.tastenortheast.co.uk*

★ Tastes of Anglia | *www.tastesofanglia.com*

★ Taste of the West | *www.tasteofthewest.co.uk*

★ South East Taste | *www.southeastenglandfoodanddrink.co.uk*

★ Food North West | *www.foodnw.co.uk*

★ London | *www.london.gov.uk/londonfood*

Index

24 Carrots, 93

A

Abel & Cole, 231
accountants, 101–102
advertising. *see also* marketing
   on Facebook, 213
   online adverts, 198
AGA, 184
airline catering, 25
Alchemist Drinks, 138–139
allergies, 142–144
Allergy UK, 143
Anderson, Alexandra, 224
angel investors, 80
Angelic Gluten-free, 58–59
Angels Den, 80
animal welfare, 6, 147
APC Couriers, 74
Asda, 227–228
Ashburton Cookery School, 41
Asiama, Christiana, 120
Association of Bakery Ingredients
  Manufacturers, 19
Astaniotis, Olga, 10, 36–37
autumn, 170
Award Intelligence, 185
awards, 185–187

B

Ball, Ruth, 138–139
Ballard, Miranda, 68, 145, 254–255
Balon, Adam, 17
banks, 76
barter, 55
Become a Blogger, 206
Bestway Cash & Carry, 139
BeuteFuchs, 39–40
BigBarn, 209, 236
Billingsgate Seafood Training
  School, 42
Blogger, 205
blogs, 11, 203–209
   content, 204–205
   platforms, 205
   title, 203
Boddy, Julia, 95–96
Booker Wholesale, 139
Boulton, Carla, 160
box schemes, 230–231
brainstorming, 33
branding, 37
   case study, 161–162
   checklist, 154–155
   company name, 92–94
   consistency, 161
   design, 151–155
   logos, 92
   packaging, 157–158
   on transport vehicles, 130–131
BRAVE, 208
Breckland Orchard, 152, 251
British Coffee Association, 19

British Franchise Association
  (BFA), 87, 88
British Hospitality Association, 143
British Library Business and IP
  Centre, 97
British Retail Consortium, 146
British Street Awards, 185
Brompton Cookery School, 42
Bruce, Sam, 78
building societies, 76
Burger King, 213
bursaries, 78
business angels, 80
business banking, 76
business cards, 188
business clients, 24
business continuity, 108, 109
business entities, 23–29, 85–88
   caterers, 23–26
   franchise model, 87–88
   limited liability partnerships, 86
   partnerships, 86
   pop-up ventures, 35
   producers, 27–29
   sole traders, 86
Business Link, 57, 69, 76, 97, 151
Business Names Act 1985, 94
Business Networking
  (International), 188
business plans, 7, 47–49, 56, 57
   case study, 58–59
business rates, 110
business skills
   accounting and tax, 101–103
   advice and guidance resources,
    43, 57, 58, 59, 78–79

business plans, 47–49, 56
  financial management, 28, 50–52
  funding the business, 72–85
  negotiation, 25, 67
  organisational, 25
  pricing, 70–71
butchery, 67
buyer behaviour, 14, 16, 55, 227–228

Cake Boss, 38
Cake Craft World, 63
capital finance, 75–82
Capper, Mel, 252–253
case studies
  Alchemist Drinks, 138–139
  Angelic Gluten-free, 58–59
  baking, 37–38
  Chokolit, 104–105
  Country Markets, 221
  Edible Ornaments, 13–15
  Foodie Bugle, The, 206–208
  FoodLovers Britain, 49
  Gourmet Vanilla, 161–162
  Growing Communities, 231
  Handmade Fudge Company, 82
  Highland Game, 184
  Innocent Drinks, 17
  Kitchen Table Talent Awards,
    126–127
  The Lawn, 252–253
  Let it Be Cake, 37–38
  marketing, 190
  Moor Farm Shop, 131–132
  More to Life than Shoes, 188–189
  Mrs Tinks, 95–96

  Mukaase Foods, 120
  Posh Pop, 152
  Scoop, 223
  Shrewsbury Bakehouse, 53–56
  South Devon Chilli Farm, 89–90
cash and carry, 139
cash flow forecasts, 51
Caterer and Hotelkeeper, 63, 209
certificate of incorporation, 76
Chambers of Commerce, 58
Child, Julia, 33
Chilled Food Association, 18
Chilli Fiesta, 238
Chokolit, 104–105
City & Guilds, 43
City Markets Glasgow, 140
cleaning equipment, 125
Coca-Cola, 17
Coeliac UK, 143
Coltman, Emily, 101
commercial premises, 54, 129
commercial scale catering, 23
community centres, 129
community finance organisations, 81
Companies Act 1985, 94
Companies House, 85, 94, 97
competitions, 183
competitors, 16, 24, 38, 52
complaints, 246
Concern Universal, 174
conferences, 24
Constant Contact, 196
contracts, 105
cooking schools, 11, 40–43
CopyBlogger, 206
copyright, 97
Cordon Vert, 42

corporate events, 24
costs, 28
  deliveries, 71–74
  equipment, 63–66
  labour, 67, 68–69
  packaging, 72, 73
  production, 28
  suppliers, 67
  transport, 130–131
  utilities, 122
council tax, 110
Country Living Magazine, 13, 63,
  126–127, 253
Country Markets, 65, 220–221
courier delivery, 72–74
Create, 193
credit cards, 77
crisis management, 109
Crowdfunder, 81
crowdfunding, 81
Cumbria Life Food and Drinks
  Awards, 187
customers
  buyer behaviour, 14, 16, 55, 227–228
  corporate, 24
  engaging with, 250
  feedback, 15, 28, 34, 246
  finding and keeping, 16
  market research, 15, 17
  needs and wants, 37
  target markets, 27, 48, 71, 166

Damer, Helen, 126–127
de Soissons, Silvana, 206–208, 212
delicatessens, 11

Delicious magazine, 209
Deliciously Yorkshire, 34
deliveries
dates, 55
   systems, 71–74
   transport, 130–131
Department of Trade and Industry (UKTI), 105
Design Council, 151, 193
Design Week, 193
designers, 152–155, 193
direct selling, 27
discounts, 25
Discover Northern Ireland, 240
distributors, 162
Doherty, Fraser, 8
domain names, 93–94, 194
Dragons' Den, 48

E

Eating Seasonably, 172–173
eBay, 63
Eckington Manor Cookery School, 41, 42
e-commerce tools, 199
economic climate, 56
Economic Development Boards, 58
Edible Ornaments, case study, 13–15
Elance, 193
elevator pitch, 15, 187
Ella's Kitchen, 92, 166–167
emails, 196–197, 198
Empire Farm, 43
employers' liability insurance, 108
English Beef and Sheep Meat, 141
English Food and Drink Alliance, 123

Enterprise Nation, 57, 75–76, 101, 194, 213
environmental accreditation, 122
environmental health, 88–89. *see also* health and safety
equipment
   checklist, 64–65
   costs, 63–65
   health and safety, 66, 125
   hire, 25, 118
   investing in, 52, 56, 66
   storage, 65
   time-saving devices, 66
   working environment, 118–119
ethical food, 173–174, 223
Ethical Trading Initiative, 174
events
   case study, 252–253
   checklist for, 240–251
   corporate, 24
   family, 24
   farmers' markets, 235–237
   food festivals, 238–251
Everall family, 131–132
expenses, 28, 101
Experimental Food Society, 139
experimentation, 11
exports, 105

F

F3 consultants, 209
Facebook, 10, 35, 81, 183, 188, 198, 212–213
Fairtrade Foundation, 173–174
Family Food reports, 18
family life, 29, 38, 95

Farm Direct, 236
farmers' markets, 11, 12, 25, 235–237
   display and catering, 241
   preparing for the event, 240
   running a stall, 244–251
   sales and marketing, 242
   supplies, 242–244
Farmers' Weekly, 235
Farrow & Ball, 121
Fat Hen, 42
Fearnley-Whittingshall, Hugh, 172
feedback, customer, 15, 28, 34, 246
festivals. *see* food festivals
Finance for Small Business, 101, 102
financial capital. *see* funding
financial management, 50–52
   accounting and tax, 101–103
   Value Added Tax (VAT), 101–103
Find Networking Events, 188
first aid, 143–144
Fish in a Box, 159
Flavours of Hertfordshire, 187
Floodlight, 43
focus groups, 33, 34
Food and Drink Federation, 19, 209, 225
Food and Farming Awards, 185
Food Blogger Connect, 206
Food Bloggers Association, UK, 206
Food Farm reports, 18
food festivals, 11, 23, 238–251
   display and catering, 241
   preparing for the event, 240
   running a stall, 244–251
   sales and marketing, 242
   supplies, 242–244
Food Funnel, 129

food labelling, 156–157
food labs, 222
Food Marketing Network, 52–53
food miles, 235
Food Network, The, 188
Food Programme (BBC), 11, 185
Food Standards Agency, 89, 91, 123, 124
Food Statistics Handbook, 18
Foodie Bugle, The, 206–208, 212
FoodLovers Britain, 12, 49, 147, 239
For Food Smokers, 67
Foundation East, 81
franchises, 87–88
Free Agent, 102
Free From Food Awards, 186
Freedom Food, 146–147
Frooition, 199
funding, 75–82
   case study, 82
   community finance organisations, 81
   credit cards, 77
   crowdfunding, 81
   grants, 75–76, 77–79
   loans, 75
   venture capital, 80
Funding Circle, 80

gaps, market, 15, 16
General Food Law Regulations, 91
Gillies, Kirsty, 58–59, 144
global trade, 105

gluten-free diets, 25, 58–59
Goddess on a Budget [blog], 208
Good Food magazine, 209
Good Housekeeping Institute, 184
Google, 197–199
Gourmet Vanilla, 161–162
Graeme Kidd Memorial Bursary, 78
Grampian Food Forum Innovation Awards, 187
grants, 75–76, 77
Great British Bake Off, 37, 38
Green, Henrietta, 12, 49
Green & Blacks, 28
green issues, 122, 228
Grocer, The, 209
Grocer Own Label Food & Drinks Awards, 186
GroovyCart, 199
Growing Communities, 231
Guild of Fine Foods, 185

H

Handmade Fudge Company, 82
Harper Adams University, 120, 129
Harrods, 34–35
health and safety, 91, 111, 123–126
   allergies and intolerances, 142–144
   environmental health, 88–89
   equipment, 66, 125
   supplier products, 136–137
health insurance, 108
Heart of England Fine Foods (HEFF), 29, 120, 122
Herbal Fusions Association, UK, 19

Highland Game, 184
HM Revenue and Customs (HMRC), 57, 102
home insurance, 108
home-made kits, 35–36
Homemade life: Stories and Recipes from my Kitchen Table, 10, 29
homeworkers' insurance, 108
homeworking, 108–112, 128
Homeworking (HSE), 111
Horsesmouth, 58
Hurricane Design, 153

I

IGD, 227–228
industrial catering, 25
ingredients, 135
   allergies and intolerances, 142–144
   locally sourced, 224
   seasonality, 25, 168–173
   suppliers, 136–137, 139–141
Innocent Drinks, case study, 17
Institute of Grocery Distribution (IGD), 13–15
insurance, 106–109, 111
intellectual property, 96–97, 155
Intellectual Property Office, 85, 97
interpersonal skills, 24
intolerances, 142–144
investment angels, 80
investors, 80
Isle of Scilly Local Action Group, 82

J

j4b Grants, 77
Jamie at Home, 87
Jump To!, 129

K

Kantar Worldpanel, 18
Kent Business School, 14
Key Note, 18
Kickstarter, 81
Kimball, Vanessa, 208
kitchen incubators, 128
Kitchen Table Talent Awards, 126–127, 185
kitchens. *see* working environment

L

labour. *see* staff
Landskills East, 79
Lantra, 78–79
Lapin Kulta Solar Kitchen, 35
Lawn, The, 252–253
Le Cordon Bleu, 42
Leadenhall Market, 138, 139
Leiths, 42
Let it Be Cake, 37–38
Levi Roots, 28
liability waivers, 107
licensed premises, 90
lighting, 119
limited liability companies, 86
limited liability partnerships, 86

Lindley, Paul, 166–167
LinkedIn, 214
LiveJournal, 205
loans, 75, 76
Local Food Direct, 72, 97
local producers, 11, 29
logos, 92, 96
Love British Food, 240
Love Food Hate Waste, 68
Ludlow Food Centre, 129, 222
Ludlow Food Festival, 78

M

Magneto, 193
MailChimp, 196
Make Cheese, 35–36
Making Local Food Work, 222
Manchester wholesale Market, 140
margins, 70–71
Market Kitchen, 78
market research, 7–18
    buyer behaviour, 14, 55
    case study, 13–15
    competition, 16
    customers, 15–16, 17
    at events, 250
    focus groups, 33, 34
    food producers, 27
    outdoor catering companies, 25–26
    reports, 18
    retailers, 218–219
    statistics reports, 7–18
    steps, 7
    supermarkets, 228–229

testing ideas, 10–11
    trend-watching, 34–35
    unique selling point, 15
marketing, 179–190
    blogging, 203–209
    case study, 190
    elevator pitch, 15, 187
    Facebook, 212–213
    LinkedIn, 214
    'local', 224
    logo design, 92
    materials, 190
    media channels, 179–182
    networking, 187–188
    newsletters, 196–197
    photographs, 25, 63
    press releases, 180–182
    single promotions, 183
    Twitter, 210–212
    unique selling point (USP), 15,
        36–37, 39–40
    videos, 214
    websites, 193–199
    word-of-mouth, 24, 38
mark-up, 70–71
Martinsen, Claire, 152
Meat and Commercial Services, 67
Meat and Livestock Commission,
    141
media channels, 11, 37, 179–182
mentors, 57–58
Mentorsme, 58
Midland Bloggers, 206
Mintel Oxygen, 18
mobile catering, 23–26
MOO cards, 190

Moonfruit, 193
More to Life than Shoes, 11–12, 188–189
Moresoda, 208
mortgage provider, 111
Mortimer Country Food Fair, 255
motivation, 28
Mrs Tinks, 95–96
Muddy Boots Food, 68, 72, 145, 254–255
Mukaase Foods, 120
My Secret Kitchen, 87

N

name, company or business, 92–94
    online domain, 93–94
    protection of, 97
Name of the Game, The, 184
National Enterprise Network, 77
National Farmers' Retail & Markets Association, 209
national food groups, 123
National Health Service, 143
national minimum wage, 69
National Trust, 172
Nationwide Caterers Association, 108
Naughty Mutt, 160
negotiation, 25, 67
neighbours, 110, 112
Net Advantage, The, 203
networking, 11, 19, 35, 48, 187–189
New Covent Garden, 140
new product development (NPD), 165–174

case study, 166–167
market research, 167–168
stages in, 165
New Spitalfields Markets, 141
Newlyn Fish Festival, 238
newsletters, 196–197
newspapers, 11, 180–182
Next Step, 43
niche, market, 7–8, 28, 38
Nolan, Mike, 6
Northern Ireland Food and Drink Association, 123

O

Observer Food Monthly awards, 186
Olive Grows, The, 10, 36–37, 96, 129
online shopping, 49, 162
    delivery systems, 72–74
    farmers' markets, 236
Open University, 43
Organic Farmers and Growers, 146–147
organic food, 141
organisational skills, 25
outdoor catering, 23–26, 235–255
overproduction, 28

P

packaging, 72, 73, 155–162
    case study, 161–162
    environmentally friendly, 158–159
    health and safety, 126
    legal requirements, 156–157
Pampered Chef, The, 88

partnerships, 38, 86
part-time working, 23
patents, 96
PayPal, 199
pay-per-click advertising, 198
pet food, 39–40
photographs, 25, 63
physical fitness, 12, 23
planning, 47–59
    business continuity, 109
    business plans, 47–49, 56
    case study, 49, 53–56
    financial plans, 51–52
planning permission, 90, 109–110
Planning Portal, 110
Plumb, Joanna, 13–14
pop-up ventures, 35
portion control, 68
Posh Pop, 152, 251
premises. *see also* working environment
    business rates, 110
    case study, 131–132
    environmental health, 88–89
    hired kitchens, 128–130
    homeworking, 109–112, 128
    legal requirements, 91, 110–111
    licensed, 90
planning permission, 90, 109–110
Prepped, 208
Press for Attention, 180
press releases, 180–182
price, 25, 37, 52, 70–71, 248–249
primary packaging, 156
Prince's Countryside Fund, 79–80
Prince's Trust, 59, 77–79

product liability insurance, 106, 107
production
 large scale, 25, 144–145
 UK statistics, 18
products
 delivery, 71
 improvement, 11
 locally sourced, 29
 market research, 14
 new product development
  (NPD), 165–174
pricing, 52
 seasonality, 168–173
 tailored for market, 71, 166, 236
 testing, 28, 55, 144–145
profit margins, 25, 48, 51, 70–71
Promofix, 241
provenance, 6
public liability insurance, 106, 107

Q

quality, 6, 8, 135
 standards and certification, 146–147
Quality Food Awards, 186
quotes, 25

R

Ramsay, Gordon, 172
Real Food Direct, 72
Real Food Store, The, 218–219
recycling, 90, 158–159
Red One, The, 92
Red Tractor, 146–147

Reed, Richard, 17
references, 25
Reggae Reggae sauce, 28
regional food groups, 34
registration, business
 check-list, 91
 company, 85–88
 environmental health, 88–90
 Value Added Tax (VAT), 102–103
restaurants, 224
retailers
 country markets, 220–221
 local, 217–220
 supermarkets, 225–229
Riverford, 231
Rockstargroup, 58
RomanCart, 199
RSPB, 172

S

Sage Pay, 199
Sager, Sheila, 53–56
Sainsbury's, 226
sales
 box schemes, 230–231
 country markets, 220–221
 delivery systems, 71–74
 direct, 27
 farmers' markets, 235–237
 fluctuations, 14
 food labs, 222
 forecasts, 51–52
 local retailers, 217–220
 restaurants, 224
 supermarkets, 225–229

 targets, 250–251
SALSA (Safe and Local Supplier), 146
samples, 25, 190, 243, 245, 249
Santana, Elsa, 38
school catering, 25
School of Artisan Food, 41
Scoop, 223
Scotland Food and Drink, 123
Scottish Excellence Awards, 187
Scottish Meat, 141
Scrummy Bites, 78
search engines, 197–198
seasonality, 25, 168–173
secondary packaging, 156
service staff, 25
Shaw, Mark, 210
Shedworking [blog], 128
Shell LiveWIRE, 59
She's Ingenious, 58, 97
shopper insight reports, 14
Shrewsbury Bakehouse, 53–56
Shropshire Granola, 224
Simply Business, 37
Simpson, Greg, 180–181
Smarta, 57, 128, 188
smartphones, 162
Smithfield Market, 140
smoked food, 67
social media, 10, 35, 36, 81, 198, 203–214
 blogs, 203–209
 Facebook, 212–213
 LinkedIn, 214
 Twitter, 210
 videos, 214

Soil Association, 141, 146, 186
solar cooking, 35
sole traders, 85
South Devon Chilli Farm, 89–90, 168
space-saving equipment, 118–119
specialisation, 9, 11
spoilage, 71
spring, 169
Springwise, 35
Squires Kitchen, 63
staff, 8–9
    costs, 67, 69
    hiring, 8, 68–69
    insurance, 108
    pay, 69
    planning, 55
    resource planning, 55
    service, 25
stakeholder agreements, 55–56
stalls, 244–251
StartUp Shropshire, 81
Stew, 208
storage, 65, 118, 126
stress, 28
Suffolk Providore, The, 72
summer, 170
SuperJam, 8
supermarkets, 225–229
suppliers, 136–137
    costs, 67
    ethical trading, 173–174
Supply Something New programme, 226
Sussex Food and Drinks Awards, 186
Sustain, 222

target markets, 27, 48, 71, 166
Taste of the West, 82, 186
Tastes of Anglia, 225
tax, 101–103
Taylor, Genevieve, 208–209
Timmis family, 131–132
Trade Marks Journal, 85
trademarks, 96
Trading Standards Institute, 157
training, 11
    cookery schools, 41–43
    vocational, 43, 67, 78–79
Transition Network, 222
transport, 130–131
    packaging for, 156
trend-watching, 34–35, 36
Trumpers Tea, 173–174
Try Meetup, 188
Tumblr, 205
Twitter, 10, 36, 81, 183, 198
Twitter Your Business, 210

UK Business Angels Association, 80
UK Herbal Fusions Association, 19
UK Trade Association, 185
underselling, 28
Unicorn Grocery, 223
Unique selling point (USP), 15, 36–37, 39–40
USP, 15, 36–37, 39–40
utility costs, 122

V

Value Added Tax (VAT), 90, 102–103
vegetarian menus, 25
venture capital, 80
Videos, 214
village halls, 129
Virtual Farmers' Market, 236
VisitBritain, 239, 240

W

Waitrose, 225–227
Wales The True Taste, 123, 187
Ward, Rob, 52–53
waste, 67–68, 90, 118
Waters, Steve, 168
websites, 93–94, 162, 193–199, 214
    advertising on, 197–199
    content, 194–196
    design, 193
    e-commerce tools, 199
    legal requirements, 197
Welsh Beef and Lamb, 141
Welsh Lamb and Beef Producers, 141
Wenlock hampers, 29
wholesalers, 139–140
Wicks, Simon, 194
winter, 168–169
Wizenberg, Molly, 10
Women's Institute (WI), 172
word-of-mouth marketing, 24, 38
WordPress, 205

working environment
  case study, 131–132
  colour schemes, 121
  commercial premises, 54
  equipment checklist, 64–65
  green issues, 122
  health and safety, 123–126
  layout, 117–119
work-life balance, 29, 38
World's Original Marmalade
  Awards, 186
Wright, John, 17

Young Entrepreneurs, 188
YouTube, 10

Z

Zen Cart, 199
Zopa, 81